WOOD PELLET AND SMOKER GRILL

Cookbook 2021

VANCOUVER
PRESS

VANCOUVER
P R E S S

CONTENTS

8

INTRODUCTION

As the name itself explains, this cookbook is written for all those people who love the idea of tasting food with a smoked flavor, the preparation of which guarantees excellent results using the wood pellet smoker grill. The wood pellet smoker grill is much more effective and functional than the simple grill, it roasts and smokes optimally. It is the ideal tool for cooking in the garden. If you want to prepare better meals using the pellet smoker grill, it is essential to understand how this appliance works, and this book was written for exactly that purpose. Let's start.

THE BASES OF THE WOODEN PELLET SMOKER GRILL

What Is A The Household Appliance Called Wood Pellet Smoker Grill?

Wood Pellet Smoker Grill is best for garden kitchen. The wood pellet smoker grill consists of several pieces: a gas grill, a kitchen oven and a charcoal smoker. The wood pellets feed the grill. Food cooked on the grill is then impregnated with the smoke from the burnt pellets. As part of the use of the indoor cooking system, it also offers the possibility of using a gas grill with integrated temperature control. To control the temperature, air flow and fire this appliance has an electronic control panel which ensures that the food does not burn. Furthermore, the recent models of wood pellet smoker grill have heat sensors that allow perfect cooking.

This type of grill is very popular for its ease of use. The wood pellets used have a thickness of about ¼ of an inch, they are very small. These pellets allow great control to maintain the cooking temperature. The pellets are available in various types of wood: cherry, apple, American walnut and others. The different woods give different aromas, different types of smoke and flavor. The food absorbs the Smokey flavor and thus gets a unique taste.
The pellets are placed in the storage hopper; in this way it is possible to respect the right dosage and obtain the perfect temperature for the desired cooking. In about 20 minutes the preparation of the grill is completed.

A Brief History

In 1970 the oil crisis increases the demand for domestic heating and the focus shifts to alternative sources, so wood pellets are invented. The pellets were initially very small, more or less the size of a capsule, and were made with sawdust. Then in 1980 the two aircraft engineers Boeing and Whitfield experimented with wood pellet ovens. Then, in 1985, the pellet grill arrived.

How Does It Work?

The functioning mechanism of the pellet flue grill is simple. First you need to add the wood pellets to the hopper, then the pellets are added to the chamber, the built-in fan supplies the air to the wood pellets, consequently the air is heated and pressurized. The glowing balls heat the chamber and the hot air and smoke created by the pellets circulate in the chambers. The ITC helps to control the cooking temperature.

IGNITION

The output power required for this appliance is 12 VDC for start-up and operation. Some parts of the grill, designed by different manufacturers, require 12 VDC from the car battery.

The A / C and D / C converter is supplied for use with 120 VAC. The power is used to operate the following parts: the auger, the igniter rod, the fan and the controller. The amount of power used by these four parts is minimal.

This grill is safe, and comes with a fire pot and a greased pan which also allow indirect cooking. The structure prevents flare-ups.

The igniter rod will extinguish when the temperature set by the controller is reached.

The PID controller turns on the rod again when the temperature drops below the minimum value for cooking a meal.

The initial burn-in is the process of the brazier activity.

The auger in 10 minutes transfers the pellets to the brazier when the hopper is full of pellets.

Ignite the pellets and set the temperature between 350 and 450 degrees F.

Leave the grill on for about 40-60 minutes.

Next, cook the food and set the pellet to do its magic.

Why Choose A Wood Pellet Smoker Grill

If you want to enjoy a barbecue during the grilling season, the only wise choice is the wood pellet smoker, which makes the meat healthy and flavorful. According to the manufacturer, the wood pellet smoker grill uses an indirect cooking technique, which considerably reduces the formation of carcinogens. Cooking meat on a gas or charcoal grill can lead to the formation of

HCAs, heterocyclic amines and PAHs, harmful substances also known as polycyclic aromatic hydrocarbons. HCAs are formed when meat is cooked at high temperatures. Most people are not clear on why it is better to use the wood pellet smoker grill. However this type of smoker grill offers the best ratio between versatility, ease of use and taste.

ADVANTAGES OF WOOD PELLET SMOKER AND GRILL

- The Smokey flavor and delicious taste.
- Easy to use.
- Give the consistent cooking result.
- The ITC (intelligent temperature control) gives the user a range and control for cooking temperature.
- It can bake, grill, and smoke with ease of access.

FOLLOWING ARE SOME OF THE REASONS TO CHOOSE THE WOOD PELLET SMOKER GRILL:

- The best wood smoke flavor
- No flare up
- Easy to use
- No hard and fast learning

- Fuel efficient
- It provides baking, grilling, smoking for one price
- No over smoking
- Very reliable and versatile equipment
- Best suitable for busy people
- It requires no transportation of propane

The Various Uses of Wood Pellet Smoker Grill

There are several smokers on the market, and to try and learn about them you need time, experience and attention. It also requires a certain economic investment, and most of these appliances are not easy to use, compared to the smoke grills we are talking about here. Gas grills are then available on the market but do not guarantee the same results.

The most important feature of this type of grill is to slowly smoke meats such as pork or brisket, or grill a great burger. It can also cook steaks at the push of a button. The button starts the grill and also controls the temperature.

The wood pellet smoker grill cooks food to make it extraordinarily tasty. The smoky flavor is definitely unmatched. Furthermore, this type of grill does not need to stay up all night, just press that button, and after a few hours go back to enjoying an exceptional dish.

This type of smoker grill offers an effortless cooking experience with the best possible result. Wood pellet smoker grills are better compared to both charcoal and gas grills. You just have to decide what you want to prepare.

It is ideal for grilling on windy days. Generally a barbecue when there is wind is hell: it is frustrating, as well as impossible to continue if the rain arrives. If you are looking for a fixture that can handle all of this, then this type of grill is what you are looking for.

The fire pot, the auger and the electronics work in synergy to release more fuel when needed and reduce the amount when not needed. So, whatever the weather conditions, the pellet is usable in any case.

This type of smoker grill warms up quickly by pressing just a button and choosing the desired temperature. The grill turns on and in a few minutes it is ready to cook. This appliance is the best accomplice of those who are very busy. Pellet grills have the convenience of gas ones, but with the extra aroma of wood.

This type of grill requires electricity to function. We do not recommend using such a grill in a humid environment. Moving parts can be subject to breakage. Therefore, it is important to make the purchase in a company so that you can take advantage of the guarantee and, if necessary, of any type of adequate technical support.

That said, there is no such appliance, with an equal level of practicality, taste and flexibility. The experience with the grills for wood pellet smokers is therefore absolutely advisable, in the full certainty that you will love this type of wood-cooked preparations.

Components:

After explaining in general the way the wood pellet smoker grill works, we now explain the individual components in more detail. This type of grid has the following components:

- Thermocouple/RTD

The feedback loop is provided to the controller by an RTD.

- Hopper

The hopper is the place where you put the wood pellets. The amount of pellet put into the hopper depends upon the cooking requirement.

- Auger

It is a built-in mechanism of the smoker grill, to transfer the pellets from the hopper to the fire pot.

- Fire Pot

It is the main area where the wood pellet burns and ignited. The hole in the fire pot house the auger, the lower center hole is for igniter rod, and the other hole is for the fan airflow.

After every cook, it is recommended to empty the fire pot from the ashes using a vacuum. It helps to increase the efficiency when cooking the next meal.

- Fan

The fan keeps burning the pellet that is in the fire pot.

- Controller

It is used to adjust the pellets flow and the air in accordance with the set point temperate.

- Heat deflector

Heat deflector is a plate that covers the fire pot. It disturbs even heat and absorbs it as well below the drip pan.

- Drip pan

It is for smoking, grilling, and cooking. It routes the grease to the grease bucket.

- Flame zone pan /drip pan

It is for grilling the food directly. It is used with other accessories like searing gates and griddles.

How To Assemble A Pro Series Wood Pellet Smoker Grill

Here are the steps that help you unpack and then assemble the grill:

1. Take everything out of the box, read the manual and check that all parts are present
2. Turn the cabinet upside down
3. Assemble the legs
4. Attach the front panel to the front and attach the side panel to the other sides
5. Attach the support bars
6. Fit the drain hose to the bottom of the cabinet.
7. Install the heat shields
8. Attach the cable bracket to the left side panel
9. Route the cable to the clip bracket on the left leg
10. Install the grease tray brackets
11. Turn the unit over
12. Attach the pellet discharge knob
13. Install the rear handles and mount the chimney at the top
14. Screw and secure the lid catch.
15. Fit the door handles
16. Install all cooking components and is ready to start cooking

3

THE DIFFERENT TYPES OF SMOKER

Electric Smokers

The electric smoker is the best ever for its ease of use. You start it, put the food in it, and finally leave the rest of the work to the smoker. There is no food that an electric smoker cannot grill: fish, poultry, meat, cheese, bread. It requires little attention, unlike other appliances that require filling the water tank, lighting wood or coal, and frequent fuel checks. The electric smoker requires only 2-4 ounces of wood chips, and in this way prepares perfect smoked foods. Furthermore, the machine maintains the temperature perfectly. On an aesthetic level, the elegant appearance and small size make it appropriate even in an apartment or condominium. With simple functions and trouble-free cooking, the electric smoker is an ideal choice even for novice cooks.

Gas Smokers

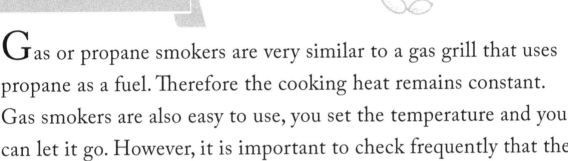

Gas or propane smokers are very similar to a gas grill that uses propane as a fuel. Therefore the cooking heat remains constant. Gas smokers are also easy to use, you set the temperature and you can let it go. However, it is important to check frequently that the fuel is not running out. On the other hand, one of the best aspects is that a gas smoker can be used when there is no electricity or when you need an oven. A gas smoker can raise the temperature up to 450 degrees, becoming even more useful for being used as an oven. Another great feature of the gas smoker is its portability which makes it usable anywhere. Just pack it up and carry it on your travels.

Charcoal Smokers

Nothing tastes better than the flavor that coal gives your food. Unfortunately, often, between setting the smoke, checking the fuel level, maintaining the temperature and checking the cooking, the whole operation can be very problematic, not to mention the risk of burning the food. These risks disappear with practice and experience. However, this type of smoker guarantees high levels of flavor.

Pellet Smokers

Pellet smokers are increasing due to their ability to maintain a constant temperature. An automated insertion system allows the cook to monitor the fuel level. The addition of the thermostat completes the ability to better control temperature and grilling. In addition, smoked food uses the heat of hard wood, giving it a delicious, rich and intense flavor. The only drawback of the pallet smoker is their high cost.

The Types Of Wood For Smoking

Wood is a fundamental element for cooking an exquisite smoked dish. Depending on the type of wood chips, the foods will in fact receive different aromas. That's why you should know which wood is best suited to the type of food you choose to cook in the smoker. The various types of wood and the characteristics that make them suitable for various types of food are illustrated below.

1- Alder: A lighter smoker wood with natural sweetness.
Best to smoke: Any fish especially salmon, poultry and game birds.

2- Maple: This smoker wood has a mild and sweet flavor. In addition, its sweet smoke gives the food a dark appearance. For better flavor, use it as a combination with alder, apple or oak smoker woods.
Best to smoke: Vegetables, cheese, and poultry.

3- Apple: A mild fruity flavor smoker wood with natural sweetness. When mixed with oak smoker wood, it gives a great flavor to food. Let food smoke for several hours as the smoke takes a while to permeate the food with the flavors.
Best to smoke: Poultry, beef, pork, lamb, and seafood.

4- Cherry: This smoker wood is an all-purpose fruity flavor wood for any type of meat. Its smoke gives the food a rich, mahogany color. Try smoking by mixing it with alder, oak, pecan and hickory smoker wood.
Best to smoke: Chicken, turkey, ham, pork, and beef.

5- Oak: Oakwood gives a medium flavor to food which is stronger compared to apple wood and cherry wood and lighter compared to hickory. This versatile smoker wood works well blended with hickory, apple, and cherry woods.

Best to smoke: Sausages, brisket, and lamb.

6- Peach and Pear: Both smoker woods are similar to each other. They give food a subtle light and fruity flavor with the addition of natural sweetness.

Best to smoke: Poultry, pork and game birds.

7- Hickory: Hickory wood infuses a strong sweet and bacon flavor into the food, especially meat cuts. Don't over smoke with this wood as it can turn the taste of food bitter.

Best to smoke: Red meat, poultry, pork shoulder, ribs.

8- Pecan: This sweet smoker wood lends the food a rich and nutty flavor. Use it with Mesquite wood to balance its sweetness.

Best to smoke: Poultry, pork.

9- Walnut: This strong flavored smoker wood is often used as a mixing wood due to its slightly bitter flavor. Use walnut wood with lighter smoke woods like pecan wood or apple wood.

Best to smoke: Red meat and game birds.

10- Grape: Grape wood chips give a sweet berry flavor to food. It's best to use these wood chips with apple wood chips.

Best to smoke: Poultry

11- Mulberry: Mulberry wood chips is similar to apple wood chips. It adds natural sweetness and gives berry finish to the food.

Best to smoke: Ham and Chicken.

VARIOUS TYPES OF CHARCOAL AND THEIR BENEFITS

Charcoal is one of the best fuels for smoking, and smoking food with charcoal is fantastic. While lighting charcoal, managing airflows, and keeping heat and temperature under control is still a challenge, the excellent taste that comes with it is worth the effort. But not all charcoals are the same and choosing one in particular is a matter of personal taste.

Lump Charcoal

Charcoal or hardwood, as the best fuel source, are the griller 's first choice. This type of coal is obtained by burning logs for a few days in an underground pit. This is how the water, sap and other substances inside the trunk burn, producing a pure coal or a piece of coal. This charcoal burns beautifully, with great heat at the beginning and less at the end; therefore charcoal is a suitable choice for cooking that involves the rapid use of the grill or to make the most of the intensity of the heat. If you then add the char, then the aroma of wood smoke will be maximized. Since the charcoal extinguishes the flame in about half an hour, it is necessary to sustain the fire to maintain the temperature; this operation takes only 5-10 minutes, and is done by adding some extinguished coal. It is advisable to use charcoal by combining different woods, such as maple, oak or walnut, and to integrate by inserting shavings of the same woods approximately every 40 minutes during the smoking process.

Charcoal Briquettes

Charcoal briquettes are actually crushed charcoal. The advantage of using this product is found in the uniformity of its shape and size, which is achieved thanks to chemical binders and fillers such as coal dust. It is very easy to create a charcoal bed with this type of briquette. The only downside to using this product is the fact that in this format and composition the coal burns faster. This fact allows you to have a short window of time to smoke, and it is still necessary to add more briquettes during grilling.

THE DIFFERENCE BETWEEN BARBECUING A MEAT AND SMOKING IT

There are mainly two extremely popular methods of cooking meat: grilling and smoking. These are different systems, which require different equipment, temperatures and cooking times. Here is a small diagram that compares these two methods.

Barbecuing Meat

Using the barbecue requires slow, indirect, low heat cooking between 200 and 250 degrees F; it is a cooking suitable for meats such as beef breast, whole pork, turkey or pork shoulder. They are tough-muscled animals that require slow cooking over low heat to enjoy moist, tender meat. The result will be incredible. You understand that the cooking is perfectly successful when the meat comes off the bone. When using the barbecue, fuel must be checked and refilled often, and this must be done quickly as lifting the lid exposes the meat to the air. This way the meat can dry or dry out.

Cooking on the barbecue requires that the grill must be heated in advance until it is hot to the right point. Then we light coals or briquettes in the quantity necessary to ensure that the fire goes out in time to allow perfect cooking. In the meantime it is necessary to season the meat; when the grill has reached temperature it is time to place the seasoned meat on it. it is essential that the grill reaches the perfect temperature.

Equipment: Fire pit, grill or a charcoal burner with lid.

Fueling: Lump wood charcoal, charcoal briquettes or wood chips combination like apple. Cherry and oak wood chips.

Best to smoke: A big cut of meats like Briskets, whole chicken, sausages, jerky, pork, and ribs.

Temperature: 190 to 300 degrees F

Timing: 2 hours to a day long.

Smoking Meat

Smoking is a very ancient cooking technique, dating back to the inhabitants of caves. Excellent method of food preservation, over time its popularity has never waned. Smoking is the best way to bring out the rich and deep flavor of the meat, which tastes heavenly when smoked to the point where it can come loose from the bone.

During smoking the food is cooked slowly, at a temperature below 200 degrees F, so it takes a long time and a lot of patience. However, this procedure gives the meat a fabulous aromatic flavor, making it soft and silky. There are three ways to smoke food: cold smoke, hot smoke and the addition of liquid smoke. Liquid smoke is currently becoming the most common and widespread of these three types. The main advantage of this system is that the aroma of the smoke can be controlled in this way; in addition, the effect of liquid smoke on meat is practically immediate.

There is also another method, called water smoking. In this case, the best machine is the water smoker, a tool specifically designed to introduce water into the smoking process. Water helps to control the temperature of the smoker and this is a perfect system if you are cooking large meat for many hours.

Equipment: A closed container or high-tech smoker.

Fueling: The container will need an external source for a smoke. Wood chips are burn to add smoky flavor to the meat. However, the frequent check should be made to monitor and adjust temperature for smoking.

Best to smoke: A big cut of meats like Briskets, whole chicken, pork, and ribs.

Temperature: 68 to 176 degrees F

Timing: 1 hour to 2 weeks

The Difference Between Cold and Hot Smoking

Instead now let's see the difference between the cold and hot smoking system: in cold smoking, the meat is cooked between 68 and 86 degrees F, to end up being not smoked but moist. This is a good way to smoke chicken breast, steak, beef, pork chops, salmon and cheese. Cold smoking rather than cooking gives it extra aroma and flavor. In fact, in this case, the meat must still be seasoned or cooked before smoking.

On the other hand, hot smoking cooks the meat completely, and while doing so it enhances its flavor to the maximum. The meat should cook until it reaches an internal temperature between 126 and 176 degrees F, and it shouldn't go up to 185 degrees F in any case, because if this happens the meat will harden, shrink and warp. Large cuts of meat such as brisket, ham, ribs and pulled pork achieve extraordinary taste when hot smoked.

The Most Important Elements Of Smoking

We can describe six important elements in order to obtain a perfect smoking.

1- **Wood chips:** they are used as fuel, alone or together with charcoal. They add exceptional flavor to the meat. However, it is good to use them only if they are suitable for the meat being prepared.

2- **Smoker:** you can choose between four types. Options include: electric smoker, charcoal smoker, gas smoker and pellet smoker.

Each type has pros and cons.

3- Smoking time: this is an essential element for an optimal result. in this regard it is necessary that the internal temperature reaches certain values, indicated above. It may take anywhere from two hours to more than two weeks.

4- Meat: in all these preparations the absolute protagonist is meat, which at the end of the smoking process must be softer, juicier and tastier than ever. The use of wood chips completes the work.

5- Rubbing: the meat should be rubbed with aromas, salt and spices, to give it greater sweetness, taste and warmth. The preparation of this mix must achieve an adequate balance of flavors.

6- Mop: Mop is the liquid that can be used for smoking meat. Gives flavor to helps maintain tenderness and moisture throughout the smoking process

OPERATION AND SAFETY

A wood pellet smoker grill is the latest trend in grilling. The use of pellets, in all its variants, represents the great innovation: from cherry to apple, from American walnut to maple, or even other types of wood. Before starting the cooking process, however, it is good to follow some safety tips.

How to Use

The wood pellet smoker grill needs to be preheated before starting the actual cooking of the food, therefore it takes time and a little patience.

The minimum grill temperature is 100 to 240 degrees F. The food is ready in a few hours, and it is very important to check it constantly.

This type of grill works the same way as any other traditional smoker. Just sit back and relax, and let the appliance work.

It is necessary to bring the smoker to the necessary temperature before baking.

Operation

Wood pellet smokers have an extremely simple functionality, even for the non-professional griller. The main feature of this grill is represented by a system of probes, one for meat, with its plug-in, one for food (to measure the internal temperature of the food) and an ICT unit that is used to constantly check the temperature. Below we present the basic steps for the operation of any wood pellet smoker. If you haven't used the appliance for a while, first clean it.

Then choose your favorite pellet and then load the tank.

Preheating must be initiated before the proper fuel flow can be adjusted.

Prepare your beef, well seasoned. Place the meat inside the grill and let the temperature rise to 225 degrees F in the cooking space. At this point you can introduce the core temperature probe into the meat, possibly reaching the center. Always try to keep your hands clean during the cooking process.

Now adjust the thermostat, so that the pellets remain at a temperature of 225 degrees F. At this temperature, a cooking time equal to one hour and thirty minutes will be required for every pound of meat. Let it cook slowly.

When the core temperature of the meat reaches 195 degrees F, you can take the meat off the grill and let it rest for an hour before cutting it.

Tips and Techniques

If you are purchasing this type of smoke grill for the first time and want to cook an excellent meal, the process may seem complicated. However, hardwood is an easy and convenient, as well as clean, solution for using the grill in the garden. And actually cooking with the wood pellet smoker grill is a very simple process since all the work is done by the same pellet.

On a practical level, the wood pellets are added to the hopper, then the temperature is selected and the grill is started. Once the grid has been programmed, the rotating auger will automatically add the pellets from the hopper, when needed.

Although this is an easy-to-use appliance, when cooking with wood pellets the most important thing is to observe possible temperature fluctuations.

Here are some cooking tips that need to be followed when using a wood pellet smoker grill:

When cooking with this type of smoker, it would be good to avoid low quality pellets, especially since it produces a large amount of ash, and this ash could disturb the temperature regulation sensors. We therefore recommend the use of high quality pellets, which provide a decidedly clean combustion and a clearly superior taste and aroma.

After use, it is essential to clean the food residues from the grill to keep the appliance in the best conditions. The use of old wood pellets is not recommended, just as it is strongly advised not to use heating pellets. Many think that heating pellets can be used instead of wood pellets for barbecues, but this is often not the case. Heating pellets are made with pine wood and are not recommended for cooking meat, due to the aroma that this type of wood gives to food.

In addition, that type of pellet contains binders that also risk compromising the quality of the meat. It is always better to use food-grade wood pellets, a product that is generally purer, cleaner and burns more quickly.

Speaking instead of the various aromas that the wood pellet can give to the meat, there are various levels of taste depending on the type of wood, from the most delicate flavors to the strongest ones: the most frequently used are walnut, apple, American walnut, maple, but there are many others.

In the context of processes such as smoking and barbecues, everything needs planning and time. When cooking this way for the first time, it is important to choose an appropriate menu. Below we will look at some other tips, useful for getting the maximum cooking experience while using a wood pellet smoker. When cooking vegetables together with meat, for example, it is recommended to add these vegetables towards the end of cooking, for a very short time. Appetizers, on the other hand, can be prepared on secondary grids.

It is essential to control the temperature of the meat during its cooking, also because the higher the temperature, the lower the smoke. Most pellets will not cause consistent smoke that is around 300 degrees Fahrenheit or higher. Therefore it is recommended to use pellets of your choice when processing and cooking foods that require higher temperatures, as the pellets will not affect the final taste.

When using this type of grate, it is advisable to keep the preparation space clean, and to cover it with cling film or aluminum foil. It is also advisable to protect the skin by wearing gloves while touching meat and spices. To make the meat juicier and softer, it is important to remember to cut the meat perpendicular to the line of the muscle fiber.

Service & Maintenance

Now we list some tips to carry out adequate maintenance for this type of grids. The first tip is to keep the appliance clean. The pellet gearmotor requires in
 actually a fairly simple maintenance, but it is necessary once in a while to clean the ash from the brazier. This can be done using any shop vacuum cleaner.

We recommend cooking every 5 meals cooked with the smoker.

- Removing sawdust with a vacuum cleaner is ideal for cleaning the area around the hopper.
- The grids must be cleaned after each use.
- We do not recommend the use of liquids or sprays to clean the inside of the smoker.
- It is strongly recommended to cover the smoker grill to keep it

it constantly protected from various atmospheric agents such as sunlight, dust, hot and cold weather.

- The most common part of this grill is a brazier which will eventually need to be replaced due to intense heat and frequent use. This brazier can be replaced with any stainless steel brazier.

How to Clean Your Wood Pellet Smoker Grill

It is very important to keep the smoker grill clean in order to give your dishes the best possible taste.

The operation of cleaning the grill is quite simple, just a few minutes are enough, immediately before and shortly after cooking, carry out this operation. A clean grill is certainly the best ally for an excellent result. To keep the grill at its best, cover the dripping pan with aluminum foil.

If, on the other hand, you prefer to avoid the use of aluminum, it is important to be sure to remove any food residue from the dripping pan, preferably after each cooking; in fact, if the dripping pan is not perfectly clean every time something else is cooked, they will ruin the flavor of what we are cooking.

To scrape and remove residues from the dripping pan, the ideal is to use a wire barbecue brush. A paper towel will do just fine for cleaning the sides.

Remove the dripping pan after each cooking and use a shop vacuum to regularly vacuum all the ash. Undoubtedly this type of grill is a highly efficient tool, however the wood pellets leave a lot of ash in the brazier, which can reduce the efficiency of the appliance.

Accessories & Tools

When cooking with a wood pellet smoker grill there are accessories that can come in handy. Here is a small list:

Meat Thermometer (Digital)

The meat probe is an element that is usually part of the appliance, but it is always better to have your own digital meat thermometer anyway.

Smoker Box

Ideal in the preparation of smoked cheese, salmon and walnuts. It acts as a chamber to keep food at room temperature.

Rib Rack

The rib grill, perfect for making large plates of ribs and barbecue ribs.

Knives

A great set of knives and scissors is essential for being able to raw and cooked meat.

Insulating gloves

You cannot ignore the use of quality rubber gloves, which help protect your hands during the various cooking operations.

Pizza Paddle

The pizza shovel allows you to cook the pizza and also helps to place or remove large pizzas.

Griddles

It can hold many delicious foods inside the grill, for example fried potatoes, eggs or pancakes.

Flavor Injectors

These tools are perfect for flavoring foods with marinades, sauces, gravies or liquids.

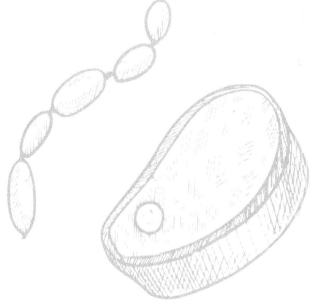

BEST FOOD SMOKING TIME TABLE

Items to Smoke	Temperature	Time for Smoking	Internal Temp	Wood Pellet Choice
Salmon	250 Degrees F	2 Hours	145 Degrees F	Alder
Chicken	350 Degrees F	30 Minutes	170 Degrees F	Pecan, Apple
Tuna	250 Degrees F	1 Hours	125 Degrees F	Apple, Oak, Cherry
Oyster	225 Degrees F	15 Minutes	To Taste	Cheery, Apples and Oak
Bell Pepper	225 Degrees F	1 Hour 30 Minutes	Until Tender	Maple
Corn	450 Degrees F	15 Minutes	Until Its Tender and Soft	Maple
Onion	250 Degrees F	2 Hours	Until Its Tender and Soft	Maple
Crab	200 Degrees F	15 Minutes	170 Degrees F	Apple
Bell Pepper	225 Degrees F	1 Hour 30 Minutes	Until Tender	Maple
Peach	225 Degrees F	35 Minutes	To Taste	Maple
Potato	440 Degrees F	25 Minutes	Until Crispy	Maple
Pineapple	250 Degrees F	1 Hours	To Taste	Maple
Squash	225 Degrees F	1 Hours	Until Tender	Maple
Sausage	225 Degrees F	1 Hour 30 Minutes	160 Degrees F	Oak, Pecan, Hickory
Lamb Chop	165 To 450 Degrees F from Smoke to Sear	10 To 20 Minutes	145 Degrees F	Cherry

Items to Smoke	Temperature	Time for Smoking	Internal Temp	Wood Pellet Choice
Lamb Rack	275 Degrees F	1 Hour 30 Minutes	145 Degrees F	Apple, Oak, Cherry
Turkey	250 Degrees F	30 Minutes	165 Degrees F	Apple
Turkey Legs	225 Degrees F	4 To 5 Hours	165 Degrees F	Apple
Baby Back Ribs	225 Degrees F	5 Hours	190 Degrees F	Hickory
Pork Shoulder	225 Degrees F	10 Hours	205 Degrees F	Hickory
Pork Chops	325 Degrees F	45 Minutes	160 Degrees F	Apple
Pork Lion	250 Degrees F	3 Hours	160 Degrees F	Apple, Oak, Hickory
Tenderloin	400 Degrees F	30 Minutes	120 Degrees F	Oak, Hickory
Texas Shoulder	250 Degrees F	12 Minutes	195 Degrees F	Oak, Hickory
Artichokes	225 Degrees F	2 Hours	165 Degrees F	Maple

5

BASIC PREPARATIONS

Choosing Smoker Grill

The most important step when talking about this type of preparation is the choice of the smoker. You can choose between various types: coal, gas or electric smoker. The charcoal smoker works for a long time, has the characteristic of keeping the heat more constant, and also gives the meat an aroma in purity. The gas smoker, on the other hand, is the perfect choice for the novice cook, since it is not necessary to monitor the temperature during the process; the downside may be that the meat will be less flavorful than that cooked with the coal system. Cooking with the electric smoker is the easiest thing in the world: you turn it on, place the meat in it and leave. In the section "types of smokers" you will find more information on this.

Choosing a Type Of Fuel

The wood shavings give the meat an exceptional, unique aroma, so it is important to choose the type that best enhances its taste. The various woods differ in intensity, some are stronger and others more delicate, some are even just enough to produce a small amount of smoke. More information can be found in the dedicated section, "Types of wood to be smoked".

Smoking Methods

To smoke the meat, you can use wet smoke, dry smoke, liquid smoke or water smoke.
In the section "The fundamental difference between cold and hot smoking" the various characteristics and differences are described. Also in the section "The difference between grilling a meat and smoking it" there is more information about it.

Soaking Wood Chips in Water

Soaking wood chips is a great way to get longer smoke production time. This is because dry wood burns quickly and there is a risk if this happens that the smoked meat is then dry. These chips are unnecessary if you need a short smoke. In the case of using the shavings, on the other hand, the ideal is to immerse them in water for about 4 hours, before starting the smoking process. Subsequently they must be drained and then wrapped and tightly closed in aluminum foil. Finally it is necessary to make small holes in the bag, using the prongs of a fork or a toothpick.

Set Smoker Grill

Each type of smoker starts differently. To start the wood or coal smoker, the first thing to do is to light half of the coals, then wait for the flame to go out. Immediately afterwards, the remaining coal is added and the wood shavings chosen are also added. After having turned them on and waiting for the time necessary for them to warm up properly, the charcoal is pushed aside and then the meat is placed on the other side of the grill. This operation causes the meat to be smoked indirectly and slowly. At this point, coal and / or shavings continue to be added to the smoker.

Instead, the gas / propane or electric smoker offers a very simple operation: just turn it on according to the guidelines of the individual manufacturer, then add the soaked wood chips and fill the water container, if the model of smoker in question has one. At that point, using the built-in thermostat or purchasing one, the internal temperature can be monitored. When the desired temperature is reached, the meat can be added.

Selecting Meat

Here are some types of meat that are perfect for cooking using smoking.

Beef: ribs, brisket and corned beef.

Pork: spare ribs, roast, shoulder, and ham.

Poultry: whole chicken, whole turkey, and big game hens.

Seafood: Salmon, scallops, trout, and lobster.

How to Prepare Meat

Prepare the meat following the instructions of the single recipe. Sometimes the meat is left to mature, at other times it is massaged thoroughly with sauces or marinades, at other times it is simply seasoned by rubbing the aromas. These preparation methods ensure that once cooked meat is tasty, fragrant, soft and juicy. The brine, on the other hand, is an exceptional solution for treating meats such as poultry, pork or ham. The procedure is based on dissolving the ingredients necessary for the preparation of the brine in water poured into a huge container, then the meat is added. This is left to soak for at least 8 hours, then it is rinsed properly, finally it is dried by gently dabbing it, and only afterwards the smoking process begins.

For types of meat such as beef or briskets, marinating with added flavorings is the right procedure. With these types of cuts it is certainly better to make some deep cuts in the meat, so that the marinade can penetrate deeply. The meat is then drained and then smoked. the meat or smoke it immediately.

Rubbing with flavorings is a more suitable procedure for treating beef, poultry or ribs. It is a combination of salt and a lot of spices, rubbed liberally all over the meat, which is then left to rest for at least 2 hours or more before moving on to the smoking process. However, before smoking the meat, it is important to make sure it is at room temperature; this thermal factor guarantees to be able to cook the meat in a uniform way and its internal temperature at the end of smoking.

Placing Meat Into the Smoker Grill

In any case, we must avoid putting the meat directly on the fire in the smoker; in fact the goal of smoking is basically to cook the meat at a low temperature. Put the smoker fuel on one side and the meat on the other side, then let it cook slowly.

As for the smoking time, this depends on the internal temperature of the meat. For this it is very useful to use a meat thermometer, inserting it in the thickest part. The smoking time can also vary depending on the size of the piece; for this reason it is important to carefully follow the recipes to be clear about the exact smoking time of the meat that you have decided to cook.

How To Baste Meat

Some recipes suggest brushing the meat with light liquids, marinades, or sauces. This is a great way to enhance the taste of the meat, and it also helps to preserve the moisture inside the meat during smoking. Always follow the recipe carefully to see if basting is needed.

How does meat extraction work instead? When the meat reaches the desired internal temperature it can be removed from the smoker. As for poultry, it must be removed from the smoker when its internal temperature is 165 degrees F. Instead if it is ham, pork and minced meat, the ideal internal temperature is around 160 degrees F. Finally. the rough guideline for the right core temperature for steaks, roasts, and ribs is 145 degrees F.

6

Menu

BEST RECIPES

BEEF RECIPES

SMOKED RIBEYE STEAKS

Prep Time: 15 Minutes
Cooking Time: 35 Minutes
Servings: 1 Person

Ingredients:
½ pound Ribeye steaks, preferably 2" thick;
at room temperature for half an hour
Steak rub, any of your favorite
Directions:
1. Preheat wood-pellet grill over low
smoke. Sprinkle the ribeye steaks with the
preferred steak rub
2. Place the coated Ribeye on wood-pellet
grill & permit smoke for 20 to 25 minutes
3. Once done; do away with the beef from
grill; adjusting the temperature of pellet
grill to 400 F
4. Place the ribeye over the pellet grill
again & sear every side for multiple five
minutes.
5. Continue to cook dinner the beef till
you get your desired doneness (Steak at a
hundred 65 F is considered to be nicely
done, 145 F is considered to be medium,
and 125 F is taken into consideration to
be rare). It's important for you to drag off
the steak from the grill approximately five
degrees before the favored temp. Wrap in
aluminum foil & let sit for a couple of
minutes then slice into portions. Serve
warm and enjoy.

Nutrition Value (per serving)

517 Calories
341 Calories from Fat
38g Total Fat
17g Saturated Fa
1.8g Polyunsaturated Fat
18g Monounsaturated Fat
154mg Cholesterol
118mg Sodium
558mg Potassium
0.3g Total Carbohydrates
0g Dietary Fiber
0g Sugars
44g Protein

BALSAMIC SOY FLANK STEAK RECIPE

Prep Time: 20 Minutes
Cooking Time: 30 Minutes
Servings: 4 Persons

Ingredients:
1 ½ pounds flank steak
3 cloves garlic, chopped
½ onion, chopped
1 tablespoon Dijon mustard
½ teaspoon black pepper
1 tablespoon dried rosemary
¼ cup each of olive oil, balsamic vinegar &
soy sauce 1 teaspoon salt
Directions:
1. For Soy Balsamic Marinade: Whisk the
garlic with onion, balsamic vinegar, olive
oil, soy sauce, rosemary, Dijon, pepper and
salt in a big-sized blending bowl.
2. Place the steak in a massive sized zip-
lock bag; upload the prepared marinade.
Seal the bag & shake the ingredients
properly (make certain that the beef pieces

are nicely covered with the prepared marinade). Place the bag in a refrigerator for overnight.

3. The subsequent day; preheat your wood-pellet grill to 350 F in advance.

4. Once done; remove the steak from bag; shake off any extra marinade (booking the excess marinade inside the bag for later use).

5. Place the covered steak on the grill & cook dinner until you get your desired doneness, for several minutes on each side. As you're cooking the meat; don't forgets to comb the pieces with the kept aside marinade. Once done; do away with the steak from grill & allow relaxation for 5 mins on a reducing board. Thinly cut the grilled steak across the grain. Serve hot and enjoy.

Nutrition Value (per serving)
423 Calories
235 Calories from Fat
26g Total Fat
7g Saturated Fat
0g Trans Fat
2g Polyunsaturated Fat
15g Monounsaturated Fat
111mg Cholesterol
1603mg Sodium
701mg Potassium
7.1g Total Carbohydrates
1.1g Dietary Fiber
3.4g Sugars
38g Protein

BEEF TENDERLOIN WITH BALSAMIC GLAZE

Prep Time: 20 Minutes

Cooking Time: 1 Hour & 20 Minutes
Servings: 4 Persons

Ingredients:
1 ½ pounds beef tenderloin; trimmed, silver skin removed Beef rub, as required; any of your favorite silver skin removed Beef rub, as required; any of your favorite

For Balsamic Reduction
3 cups balsamic vinegar
3 tablespoons rosemary, fresh, finely chopped
1/3 cup brown sugar
3-4 tablespoons softened butter, at room temperature
3 garlic cloves; peeled & crushed Pepper & salt, to taste

Directions:
1. For flippantly cooking; fold the tail (chain portion) over & secure it with toothpicks or butcher's twine then, season with your favorite beef rub.

2. Set your wood pellet smoker grill to 250 F in advance. Once done; prepare dinner the tenderloin until the beef reflects an inner temperature of one hundred ten to one hundred fifteen F, for an hour, preferably on the lowest rack. Remove the meat & permit relaxation. In the meantime; set your grill temperature to 500 F. Once done; area the partly cooked tenderloin on the searing rack and prepare dinner until the meat reflects an inner temperature of one hundred thirty F, for a minute on each side.

3. Remove the tenderloin & vicinity it on a clean, large-sized reducing board & relaxation for a couple of minutes earlier than slicing. Slice into favored strips. Serve immediately; drizzled with the organized

immediately; drizzled with the organized balsamic reduction on top & enjoy.

For Balsamic Reduction
Over moderate heat in a large saucepan; combine the entire ingredients together until mixed well, for a couple of minutes.

Nutrition Value (per serving)
802 Calories
439 Calories from Fat
49g Total Fat
23g Saturated Fat
0.5g Trans Fat
1.9g Polyunsaturated Fat
19g Monounsaturated Fat
150mg Cholesterol
224mg Sodium
778mg Potassium
49g Total Carbohydrates
0.3g Dietary Fiber
44g Sugars
32g Protein

BUTTER BEEF TENDERLOIN

Prep Time: 20 Minutes
Cooking Time: 55 Minutes
Servings: 8 Persons

Ingredients:
4 to 5 pounds' beef tenderloin
2 tablespoons Worcestershire sauce
½ cup softened butter, at room temperature
2 teaspoons fresh rosemary, finely chopped
4 garlic cloves, minced
2 tablespoons course ground mustard
1 teaspoon each of black pepper & kosher salt
Directions:

1. Preheat your wood pellet grill to high heat in advance.
2. Cream the butter with Worcestershire sauce, garlic, rosemary, mustard, pepper and salt in a massive-sized mixing bowl.
3. Pat the tenderloin dry & cowl them with the organized butter mixture completely; pressing the pieces softly into the combination to adhere.
4. Let stand for half of an hour at room temperature and then, place the lined tenderloin over the hot grill grate.
5. Roast for 15 minutes on high-warmth; lower the temperature to high smoke & smoke until you get your preferred doneness, internal temperature has to reflect somewhere a hundred thirty F.
6. Remove from the pellet grill & allow stand for 7 to 10 minutes then slice into desired portions.

Nutrition Value (per serving)
891 Calories
666 Calories from Fat
74g Total Fat
33g Saturated Fat
0.5g Trans Fat
3.1g Polyunsaturated Fat
30g Monounsaturated Fat
229mg Cholesterol
513mg Sodium
900mg Potassium
1.4g Total Carbohydrates
0.4g Dietary Fiber
0.3g Sugars 52g Protein

Prep Time: 20 Minutes
Cooking Time: 1 Hour & 20 Minutes
Servings: 8 Persons

Ingredients:
1 whole beef tenderloin, trimmed (roughly 4 pounds)
1 to 2 tablespoons extra virgin olive oil, plus more for basting
Freshly ground or cracked black pepper
Vegetable oil, for oiling the rack
Coarse salt or smoked salt (kosher or sea)

Directions:
1. Set up your wood pellet smoker & preheat it to 225 F to 250 F in advance.
2. Place the meat on a huge-sized rimmed baking sheet & generously season with pepper and salt on all sides. Next, drizzle the tenderloin with olive oil on all aspects, rubbing well.
3. Place the lined tenderloin on the smoker & smoke for 45 to 60 minutes, until the internal temperature of the beef reflects 110 F. Transfer it to a massive platter & allow rest for a couple of minutes.
4. In the meantime, set up your grill & preheat to high (for direct grilling). Brush & oil the grill grate.
5. five. Transfer the tenderloin to the hot grill. Direct grill for a couple of minutes, till all sides are dark, crusty, and sizzling and the internal temperature of the meat displays one hundred thirty to 135 F (for medium-rare) or a hundred and twenty to 125 F (for rare pork); rotating the beef like a log. As it grills; don't overlook to brush the cooked tenderloin with extra of olive oil & turning the pieces halfway in the course of the grilling process till grill marks appear.
6. Place the cooked tenderloin on a clean, massive-sized slicing board & do away with the strings. Cut the meat crosswise into ¼ to ½" thick slices.

Nutrition Value (per serving)
652 Calories
476 Calories from Fat
53g Total Fat
21g Saturated Fat
0g Trans Fat
2.3g Polyunsaturated Fat
23g Monounsaturated Fat
159mg Cholesterol
111mg Sodium
693mg Potassium
0.2g Total Carbohydrates
0.1g Dietary Fiber
0g Sugars
41g Protein

PORK RECIPES

SMOKED PORK BELLY

Prep Time: 15 Minutes
Cooking Time: 4 Hours & 15 Minutes Servings: 10 Persons

Ingredients:
3 to 5 pounds' pork belly
Smoked paprika, pepper & salt to taste
Directions:

1. Preheat your pellet grill over high smoke.
2. Once done; rating the fat cap then, generously season with smoked paprika, pepper & salt.
3. Smoke for 4 hours, till the inner temperature of meat displays a hundred 65 F.
4. Remove the cooked meat from grill & allow rest for eight to 10 minutes then, reduce into individual portions; serve hot and enjoy.

Nutrition Value (per serving)
175 Calories
1082 Calories from Fat
120g Total Fat
44g Saturated Fat
0g Trans Fat
13g Polyunsaturated Fat
56g Monounsaturated Fat
163mg Cholesterol
73mg Sodium
425mg Potassium
0.1g Total Carbohydrates
0.1g Dietary Fiber
0g Sugars
21g Protein

DELICIOUS PORK SANDWICH

Prep Time: 15 Minutes
Cooking Time: 4 Hours & 15
Minutes Servings: 10 Persons

Ingredients:
For The Cuban Sandwich
1 ½ pounds roasted pork, sliced
1-pound Swiss cheese, sliced

1 ½ pounds deli ham, sliced
Dill pickles, sliced lengthwise
8 Cuban rolls, sliced lengthwise
½ stick unsalted butter, softened
3 tablespoons yellow mustard or more to taste
For The Roasted Pork
6-8 pounds' boneless pork shoulder
2 heads of garlic, roughly chopped
2 2/3 cups lime juice
2 onions, cut into rings
1 tablespoon cumin
2 tablespoons oregano
4 cups orange juice
1 tablespoon black pepper
3 tablespoons salt
Directions:
For The Roasted Pork
1. Combine the entire ingredients (don't uploads the beef shoulder) in a large-sized mixing bowl. Season the red meat butt with pepper and salt; cowl the meat with the organized marinade. Cover & permit refrigerate for overnight.
2. The next day; eliminate the red meat butt & vicinity them in high sided pan or casserole dish. Strain the marinade & add the liquid to the meat.
3. Smoke till meat displays the inner temperature as 205 F, for 10 to 12 hours, at excessive smoke.
4. Remove the red meat butt & permit rest then, pull the pork apart.
For The Sandwiches
Evenly spread the mustard on the roll, on both sides. Add the cooked red meat after which, upload cheese, ham & pickle. Top with pinnacle bun & then, wrap in an aluminum foil. Place the wrapped sandwiches over a grill; grill for multiple

mins, until the cheese is completely melted, over medium warmness; urgent the sandwiches with a forged iron skillet. Get rid of the foil & butter the sandwich on each sides. Place it over the grill once more & brown each side until you get your desired degree of doneness then, cast off from the grill & enjoy.

Nutrition Value (per serving)
607 Calories
400 Calories from Fat
44g Total Fat
21g Saturated Fat
0.6g Trans Fat
2.9g Polyunsaturated Fat
15g Monounsaturated Fat
179mg Cholesterol
1288mg Sodium
744mg Potassium
1.4g Total Carbohydrates
0g Dietary Fiber
0.1g Sugars 50g Protein

GRILLED PORK RIBS WITH GOCHUJANG BARBECUE SAUCE

Ingredients:
⅔ cup of apple cider vinegar
½ cup brown sugar
6 tbsp. gochujang (Korean hot pepper paste)
¼ cup of adobo (from a can of chipotle chiles)
2 racks St. Louis-style pork spareribs
Kosher salt and grounded pepper vegetable oil

Directions:
1. Set up the grill for 350°. Whisk vinegar, the brown sugar, gochujang paste, and the adobo in a medium bowl till sugar is dissolved. Place 1/2 of the sauce into a small bowl after which set aside.
2. Season the ribs with salt and down to earth pepper. Place every rack on a double layer of foil and wrap it up. Put them on a rimmed baking sheet and bake until they emerge as very tender however no longer falling apart, approximately 2½–3 hours. Let it cool.
3. Set up the grill for medium-excessive heat, then oil the grate. Grill the ribs, turning them several times and begin to baste with the remaining sauce until charred and lined with a thick layer of glaze, up to 8 or 10 minutes. Then positioned the ribs onto a slicing board and reduce among bones into individual ribs.
4. To be served with sauce alongside.

SMOKED PORK RIBS

Prep Time: 20 Minutes
Cooking Time: 6 Hours & 20
Minutes Servings: 6 Persons

Ingredients:
3 racks baby back ribs
1 ½ tablespoon mustard
BBQ Rub, any of your favorite
1 ½ tablespoon maple syrup
½ cup apple juice
Coarse salt
<u>For Glaze</u>
1 cup ketchup
¼ cup maple syrup
3 tablespoons hot sauce
1 teaspoon pepper

3 tablespoons vinegar
½ cup mustard
Directions:
1. Rinse the ribs & then, patting them dry the usage of a paper towel. Score the silver skin (membrane) at the concave side of the ribs; peel it off using a paper towel. Generously season the ribs with salt after which, permit the brine to dry for an hour.
2. Combine the apple juice with maple syrup and mustard in a sprig bottle. Combine the whole glaze ingredients together in a medium sized bowl; set the aggregate aside till equipped to use.
3. three. Preheat your pellet grill with excessive smoke. Once you've got brined the ribs have for one hour; spritz them with the organized aggregate within the spray bottle. Cover the ribs absolutely with the organized rub & put them in a smoker; cook dinner for three hours. Once done; spread the glaze on pinnacle of the ribs & cover them in an aluminum foil; continue to smoke for 2 greater hours. Get rid of the foil & prepare dinner for an hour; don't neglect to spread a few more glaze on pinnacle of the meat. Serve warm and enjoy.

Nutrition Value (per serving)
595 Calories
323 Calories from Fat
36g Total Fat
13g Saturated Fat
0.3g Trans Fat
5.9g Polyunsaturated Fat
15g Monounsaturated Fat
146mg Cholesterol
719mg Sodium
597mg Potassium

24g Total Carbohydrates
0.9g Dietary Fiber
19g Sugars
42g Protein

GRILLED PORK CHOPS WITH PLUMS, HALLOUMI CHEESE, AND LEMON

Ingredients:
4 tbsp. of extra virgin olive oil and more for the grill
1 tsp of honey
4 bone-in pork rib chops (1" thick)
Kosher salt and grounded pepper
4 ripe medium red or black halved plums
1 lemon, halved and seeds removed
8 oz. Halloumi cheese, ½"thick sliced
2 tbs. oregano
Aleppo style or crushed red pepper flakes
Directions:
1. Set up the grill for medium excessive warmth and oil the grate. Mix the honey and a couple of tbsp. of oil in a resalable plastic bag. Season the red meat chops with salt and level-headed pepper and positioned it into the bag. Seal it, urgent out the air.
2. Put the plums, lemon, and Halloumi on a rimmed baking sheet and spoon with tbsp. of oil. Season the plums and lemon with salt, then season everything with pepper.
3. Grill the red meat over medium high warmth, frequently turning with a pair of lengthy tongs and move it around if required to keep away from flare-ups, till an instant-examine thermometer inserted into the middle (about ½" from the bone) registers 130°, about 6–8 minutes. Place

onto a board and permit it relaxation for ten minutes. In the meantime, grill the plums, lemon, and Halloumi, turning plums and cheese once or twice, till grill marks appear and plums start to unharness their juices, approximately 4 minutes. Move the plums, lemon, and Halloumi onto the board with the red meat and let it cool for one minute. Slice each halved plum into three wedges and tear the Halloumi into portions.

4. Cut the red meat away from bone into ½" thick slices. Put the meat on plates and discard the bones. Spoon plums and Halloumi around and on pinnacle. Squeeze the juice from the grilled lemon over, then season with a lot of salt and down to earth pepper, with oregano, sprinkle with some Aleppo style pepper, and with a touch of oil.

SMOKED BRAIDED PORK LOIN

Prep Time: 20 Minutes
Cooking Time: 2 Hours & 55 Minutes
Servings: 8 Persons

Ingredients:
4 to 5-pound spork loin
Mango Chipotle Seasoning
Olive oil
1 wooden kabob skewer

Directions:
1. Rinse the pork loin and then, pat them dry the usage of paper towels.
2. To braid; make two cuts lengthwise on the loin (you need to have be having 3 related strands). Cut the loin lengthwise & all the manner thru.

3. Pour and rub a small amount of olive oil over the loin then, coat the beef with the beef rubs, any of your favorite.
4. four. Next, braid the red meat portions together after which, take a wood skewer; stick via the ends of pieces.
5. Preheat the grill of your wood pellets over Hi Smoke for a couple of mins. Place the coated loin over the grill & cook dinner for an hour. Once done; turn the warmth to 275 F & maintain to prepare dinner till the internal temperature of the beef reflects 145 F. Pull off the grill after which, wrap in aluminum foil; permit the loin to rest for 12 to 15 minutes. Slice & enjoy.

Nutrition Value (per serving)
891 Calories
666 Calories from Fat
74g Total Fat
33g Saturated Fat
0.5g Trans Fat
3.1g Polyunsaturated Fat
30g Monounsaturated Fat
229mg Cholesterol
513mg Sodium
900mg Potassium
1.4g Total Carbohydrates
0.4g Dietary Fiber
0.3g Sugars 52g Protein

STICKY SWEET GRILLED PORK SHOULDER

Prep Time: 20 Minutes
Cooking Time: 2 Hours & 55 Minutes
Servings: 8 Persons

Ingredients:

Pork
2 peeled heads of garlic
1 wide 6" piece ginger, peeled and chopped
1 cup hoisin sauce
¾ cup of fish sauce
⅔ cup of honey
⅔ cup Shaoxing wine (from Chinese rice)
½ cup chili oil
⅓ cup oyster sauce
⅓ cup of toasted sesame oil
1 4–5lb skinless, boneless pork shoulder
(Boston butt)
Kosher salt
Glaze and Assembly
¾ cup (packed) brown sugar
1 tbsps. mild-flavored molasses bread and
butter pickles, cilantro, rinsed sliced white
onion and white bread

Directions:

1. Blend the garlic, ginger, the hoisin sauce, the fish sauce, the honey, wine, the chili oil, oyster sauce, and vegetable oil in a blender until very smooth. Place 1½ cups in a little bowl for the glaze and chill. Pour the ultimate marinade right into a resalable plastic bag.

2. Put the red meat shoulder, fats side down, on a cutting board. Using a sharp knife make a shallow reduce on the whole period of the shoulder. Keep cutting deeper into the beef, lifting, and unfurling along till it lies flat. Add the portions into the bag with marinade and seal it, pressing out the air. Chill for at least 8 hours and up to at least one day.

3. Set up the grill for medium warmness.

4. Take off the beef from marinade and drip off the excess. Season anywhere with salt. Grill the beef on the cooler area of the grill so as to keep away from flare-ups.

excessive. Continue grilling the pork until an instant-examine thermometer inserted into the thickest element registers 140°–145°. Place onto a board and permit it relaxation for at the very least twenty mins.

5. Do Ahead: Pork can be grilled two days ahead. Let it cool, cowl, and chill.

Glaze and Assembly

1. Boil the brown sugar, molasses, and reserved marinade in a massive saucepan. Cook till reduced by 1/2, approximately 6 or eight mins.

2. Set up the grill for medium-high warmness or use a standard grill. Grill the red meat, basting and turning with pairs of tongs each minute, till thickly covered with a glaze, lightly burned in spots and cooked thru (an instant-study thermometer inserted into the thickest part should sign up 130°– 145°, about 6–8 mins. Place onto a slicing board and reduce against the grain (approximately ¼" thick). Serve with pickles, bread, cilantro, and onion.

SMOKED MUSTARD & BROWN SUGAR HAM

Prep Time: 20 Minutes
Cooking Time: 4 Hours & 20 Minutes
Servings: 12 Persons

Ingredients:
12 to 15 pound cured ham
Pineapple juice for basting
1-pound brown sugar
Fruit or apple hardwood pellets
1 bottle Dijon mustard

Directions:

1. Preheat your pellet smoker or pellet grill over 225 F in advance. Unwrap the

ham & cast off any excess moisture using paper towel.

2. Coat the ham with Dijon mustard then, dust the ham gently with the brown sugar. Place the coated ham in the pellet smoker / grill & smoke for 2 hours.

3. Once done, cast off the ham from pellet grill & area it over aluminum foil sheet. Baste the ham with some pineapple juice. Once you have got basted the ham; wrap it in the aluminum foil & region it over the pellet grill once more; retain to prepare dinner at 225 F for an hour greater.

4. Once done, glaze the ham. Unwrap the pinnacle of ham; make certain that you permit it sitting within the aluminum foil. Once done, closely sprinkle the meat with brown sugar & baste with the pineapple juice. Place the ham lower back over the pellet smoker or grill once more and cook at 225 F until the inner temperature of the meat reflects 145 F, for 1 hour; allow the juice and sugar to prepare your glaze.

5. Remove the ham from pellet smoker or grill & loosely tent it with aluminum foil; permit it rest for a couple of minutes. Serve warm and enjoy.

Nutrition Value (per serving)
890 Calories
343 Calories from Fat
38g Total Fat
12g Saturated Fat
0g Trans Fat
4.2g Polyunsaturated Fat
18g Monounsaturated Fat
240mg Cholesterol 5819mg Sodium
1425mg Potassium
50g Total Carbohydrates
0.1g Dietary Fiber

39g Sugars
83g Protein

LAMB RECIPES

GREEK STYLE ROAST LEG OF LAMB

Prep Time: 25 Minutes
Cooking Time: 1 Hour & 35 Minutes
Servings: 12 Persons

Ingredients:
6 tablespoons extra-virgin olive oil
1 Leg of lamb (6 to 7 pounds), bone-in
Juice of 2 lemons, freshly squeezed
2 sprigs of fresh rosemary, stems discarded, stripped needles
1 sprig of fresh oregano, or 1 teaspoon Dried
8 garlic cloves
Freshly ground black pepper & kosher salt (coarse) as required

Directions:
1. Make a series of small slits within the meat using a sharp paring knife.
2. For herb & garlic paste: Finely mince the rosemary with oregano, and garlic the use of a chef's knife on a clean, big reducing board. Alternatively, upload these substances in a meals processor.
3. Stuff some of the prepared paste into every of the slits on meat; ensure which you upload it into the slit the usage of any of the utensils. Next, upload the coated lamb on a rack, preferably inner a

large roasting pan. For easier smooth-up;
don't forgets about to line the pan with
aluminum foil.

4. Rub the outside of meat first with the
freshly squeezed lemon juice after which
with the olive oil. Using a plastic wrap;
cowl & refrigerate for overnight.

5. The next day; dispose of the meat from
refrigerator & allow sit down at room
temperature for 1/2 an hour.

6. Get rid of the plastic wrap & season the
beef with pepper and salt to taste. When
ready, preheat the grill of wooden pellet on
Smoke for four to 5 mins, with the lid
open. Set the cooking temperature to four
hundred F and near the lid.

7. Roast the lamb for half an hour.
Decrease the heat to 350 F & keep
cooking for an hour extra, until the inner
temperature of the meat reflects 140 F.

8. Transfer the cooked lamb to a huge,
clean slicing board & allow rest for a
couple of minutes then, slice diagonally
into skinny slices. Serve even as
nevertheless hot and enjoy.

Nutrition Value (per serving)
769 Calories
575 Calories from Fat
64g Total Fat
26g Saturated Fat
0g Trans Fat
5.2g Polyunsaturated Fat
28g Monounsaturated Fat
191mg Cholesterol
154mg Sodium
618mg Potassium
0.7g Total Carbohydrates
0.1g Dietary Fiber
0g Sugars 45g Protein

ROSEMARY LAMB

Prep Time: 20 Minutes
Cooking Time: 3 Hours & 10 Minutes
Servings: 2 Persons

Ingredients:
1 rack lamb, rib
A bunch of fresh asparagus
2 rosemary, springs
1 dozen baby potato
2 tablespoons olive oil
Pepper & salt to taste
½ cup butter d

Directions:
1. 1. Preheat the grill of your wood pellet to
225 F in advance.

2. Get rid of the membrane from the back
side of the ribs after which, drizzle on each
sides with olive oil; finally sprinkle with
the rosemary.

3. Combine the butter with potatoes in a
deep baking dish.

4. Place the rack of prepared ribs alongside
the dish of potatoes on the grates. Smoke
till the inner temperature of the meat
displays a hundred 45 F, for three hours.
During the remaining 15 minutes of
cooking don't neglect to add asparagus
to the potatoes & hold to cook until turn
tender.

5. Slice the lamb into desired portions &
serve with cooked asparagus and potatoes.

Nutrition Value (per serving)
668 Calories
516 Calories from Fat
57g Total Fat
27g Saturated Fat
0.9g Trans Fat

3.6g Polyunsaturated Fat
22g Monounsaturated Fat
150mg Cholesterol
256mg Sodium
665mg Potassium
17g Total Carbohydrates
2.3g Dietary Fiber
0.8g Sugars 22g Protein

SPICE MARINATED AND GRILLED LAMB CHOPS

Ingredients:
½ tsp fennel seeds
1 grated serrano chili
1 2inch piece of ginger, finely grated
4 finely grated garlic cloves
¼ cup sour cream
2 tbsp. fresh lime juice
1 tbsp. mustard oil (optional)
1 tsp dried mango powder
1 tsp dried fenugreek leaves
1 tsp grounded black pepper
½ tsp of finely grated nutmeg
1 tsp Kashmiri chili powder or paprika
2 tbsps. vegetable oil and more for the grill
12 lamb rib chops (about 2¼ pounds)
Kosher salt mint leaves, cilantro leaves, and lemon wed
ges
Special Equipment
A spice mill or mortar and pestle
Directions:
1. Toast the fennel seeds in a dry little skillet over medium warmness, often shaking, for about 45 seconds, then let it cool. Finely fall apart them with the spice mill or with mortar and pestle. Move into a huge bowl, positioned in the chili,

ginger, garlic, the sour cream, lime juice, mustard oil (if utilizing), mango powder (if utilizing), fenugreek leaves, the pepper, nutmeg, 1 tsp stew powder and 2 tbsp. of vegetable oil and blend nicely. Season the lamb chops with salt and upload to the marinade. Cover and relax for a minimum of one hour.
2. Let the lamb chops take a seat at room temperature for one hour before grilling. Set up the grill for medium heat and oil the grate. Grill the lamb for about three minutes for each side. Move onto a platter and let it rest for five to 10 minutes.
3. Top the lamb with mint and cilantro and additional chili powder. Serve it with lemon wedges.
4. Do Ahead: The lamb can be marinated 12 hours beforehand. Keep it chilled.

SMOKED RACK OF LAMB

Prep Time: 20 Minutes
Cooking Time: 1 Hour & 20 Minutes
Servings: 4 Persons

Ingredients:
A rack of lamb, preferably 4 to 5 pounds
For Marinade
1 medium lemon
4 garlic cloves, minced
1 teaspoon thyme
¼ cup balsamic vinegar
1 teaspoon basil
1 teaspoon each of pepper & salt
For Glaze
2 tablespoons soy sauce
¼ cup Dijon mustard
2 tablespoons Worcestershire sauce
¼ cup dry red wine

Directions:

1. Combine the whole marinade components together in a gallon-sized zip lock bag. Once done, trim the silver skin from the lamb racks and then, upload the trimmed racks into the gallon bag with the marinade; blend the pieces well & refrigerate for overnight.

2. The next day, preheat your wood pellet to three hundred F in advance. In the meantime, combine the entire glaze elements together in a large sized blending bowl.

3. Once the glaze is mixed and the grill is preheated, place the rack of lamb over the recent grill. Cook the racks for 12 to 15 mins and then, baste with the organized glaze aggregate; flip & cook the meat until the inner temperature displays somewhere between 135 to 145 F, about for an hour; don't neglect to baste the beef with the glaze after each half of an hour. Once done, eliminate the beef from grill & let sit down for a few minutes. Once done, cut the meat into favored portions; serve warm & enjoy.

Nutrition Value (per serving)
788 Calories
554 Calories from Fat
62g Total Fat
27g Saturated Fat
0g Trans Fat
4.9g Polyunsaturated Fat
25g Monounsaturated Fat
204mg Cholesterol
630mg Sodium
755mg Potassium
4.5g Total Carbohydrates
0.7g Dietary Fiber

2g Sugars 49g Protein

GRILLED ROSEMARY LAMB WITH JUICY TOMATOES

Ingredients:

Lamb and Sauce
1 3–4lb of boneless lamb shoulder
Kosher salt and grounded pepper
2 chopped red onions
1 bunch of rosemary leaves
1 bunch oregano leaves
¾ cup of red wine vinegar
¼ cup of extra virgin olive oil
1 cup plain whole-milk Greek yogurt
¼ cup of fresh lemon juice
1 grated garlic clove
Tomatoes and Assembly
5 beefsteak tomatoes (about 4 lb.)
sea salt flakes grounded black pepper
3 tbsp. of fresh lemon juice
1 halved red onion, thinly sliced
extra virgin olive oil

Directions:

Lamb and Sauce

1. Put the lamb shoulder, cut side up, on a slicing board. Use a sharp knife to separate the beef into smaller portions along its herbal seams, you should discover yourself with five or 1/2 dozen pieces of assorted sizes. Put the lamb into a tumbler baking dish and season with salt and grounded pepper.

2. Mix the onions, rosemary leaves, and oregano leaves till finely chopped. Add the vinegar and the oil and blend till tough purée forms. Season the marinade with salt and pepper, then pour it over the lamb pieces. Cover and allow it take

a seat for 2 or three hours.

3. Mix the yogurt, the lemon juice, and garlic in a medium bowl. Season the sauce with salt and pepper, then cowl and relax.

4. Do Ahead: Lamb may be seasoned one day in advance and the sauce-eight hours ahead.

Tomatoes and Assembly

1. Before grilling, slice the tomatoes into ½"thick rounds and put them onto a platter. Season with salt and black pepper, then drizzle with 1/2 of the lemon juice. Add onion, season with salt and pepper and drizzle the ultimate juice over, unfold rosemary sprigs on to then placed apart.

2. Set up the grill for medium warmness. Put the larger pieces of lamb onto the grate and grill till the lowest is well brown, about five minutes. Spoon some remaining marinade over the lamb, flip and keep grilling, turning every five mins until the lamb is singed in spots and well browned.

3. After a quarter-hour greater or much less, also upload the smaller pieces to the grill and comply with the same instructions. They take less time to cook. The instant read thermometer inserted into the middle of every piece must register a hundred and forty° for large portions. Begin checking the smaller ones after 7 to 10 minutes. As every bit finishes, circulate onto a platter, spreading on the rosemary. Let it rest for at the least 20 or 30 minutes.

4. Move the lamb onto a reducing board and add rosemary sprigs on the perimeters of the platter. Tip the platter just so gathered tomato and lamb juices pool at one cease and spoon over the tomatoes. With a pointy knife, slice the lamb into skinny portions and add onion and tomatoes: season with salt and drizzle with oil.

5. Sprinkle with the yogurt sauce and additional virgin oil and serve.

SMOKED LAMB CHOPS (LOLLIPOPS)

Prep Time: 20 Minutes
Cooking Time: 55 Minutes
Servings: 4 Persons

Ingredients:
2 tablespoons fresh sage
1 rack of lamb
2 garlic cloves, large, roughly chopped
1 tablespoon fresh thyme
3 sprigs of fresh rosemary, approximately 2 tablespoons
¼ cup olive oil
2 tablespoons shallots, roughly chopped
1 tablespoon honey
½ teaspoon each of course ground pepper & salt

Directions:
1. Using a fruit wood; preheat your smoker to 225 F in advance.

2. Trim any silver pores and skin & excess fats from the rack of lamb.

3. Thoroughly combine the leftover ingredients collectively (for the herb paste) in a food processor & liberally practice the paste over the rack of lamb.

4. Place the covered lamb at the preheated smoker & cook till the internal temperature of the rack of lamb displays

120 F, for 45 minutes to 55 minutes. Remove the beef & prepare your smoker or grill for direct warmness now.

5. Sear the lamb for a few minutes on every side. Let rest for five minutes after which, slice into person lollipops; serve warm & enjoy.

Nutrition Value (per serving)
184 Calories
148 Calories from Fat
16g Total Fat
3.3g Saturated Fat
0.2g Trans Fat
1.6g Polyunsaturated Fat
11g Monounsaturated Fat
12mg Cholesterol
12mg ill Sodium
75mg Potassium
6g Total Carbohydrates
0.4g Dietary Fiber
4.7g Sugars 4.2g Protein

SEVEN SPICE GRILLED LAMB CHOPS WITH PARSLEY SALAD

Ingredients:
1 cup plain whole milk yogurt (not Greek)
1 tsp grounded black pepper
1 tsp ground coriander
1 tsp ground cumin
1 tsp paprika
½ tsp ground cardamom
½ tsp ground cinnamon
½ tsp ground nutmeg
12 untrimmed lamb rib chops (about three lb.), patted dry
Kosher salt
1 thinly sliced small red onion

1 cup coarsely chopped parsley
1 tbsps. of fresh lemon juice
2 tsp sumac

Directions:
1. Mix the yogurt, grounded black pepper, coriander, the cumin, paprika, the cardamom, cinnamon, and nutmeg in a big bowl.
2. Season the 2 facets of lamb chops with salt and add onto the bowl with marinade. Turn lamb in marinade, cowl, and kick back for at the least 3 hours and no greater than 12 hours.
3. Let the lamb sit down at room temperature for one hour earlier than grilling.
4. Set up the grill for medium-high warmness. Grill the lamb, around three mins for each aspect, and let it rest five or 10 mins.
5. In the meantime, blend the onion, parsley, the lemon juice and sumac with a touch of salt in a medium bowl. Serve the lamb chops with parsley salad on top.

SMOKED LOIN LAMB CHOPS

Prep Time: 20 Minutes
Cooking Time: 1 Hour & 20 Minutes
Servings: 6 Persons

Ingredients:
10 to 12 Lamb loin chops
Jeff's Original rub recipe
Rosemary, finely chopped
Olive oil
Coarse kosher salt
Directions:
1. Place the chops on a cookie sheet or

cooling rack.

2. To dry brine, generously sprinkle the pinnacle of chops with salt.

3. Place in a refrigerator for an hour or two.

4. Once done; put off the coated meat from fridge; ensure that you don't rinse the meat.

5. Prepare an infusion of olive oil and rosemary by pouring about ¼ cup of the olive oil on pinnacle of 1 tablespoon of the chopped rosemary; set the combination apart and let sit for an hour.

6. Brush the organized aggregate on pinnacle & facets of your lamb chops.

7. Generously sprinkle the pinnacle, aspects and bottom of chops with the rub.

8. Preheat your smoker at 225 F on oblique heat.

9. For outstanding results, ensure which you use a combination of apple and pecan for smoke.

10. Cook the lined chops for forty to 50 mins, until the internal temperature of chops displays 138 F.

11. Let relaxation on the counter for 5 to 7 minutes, with foil tented.

12. Serve warm and enjoy.

Nutrition Value (per serving)
652 Calories
476 Calories from Fat
53g Total Fat
21g Saturated Fat
0g Trans Fat
2.3g Polyunsaturated Fat
23g Monounsaturated Fat
159mg Cholesterol
111mg Sodium
693mg Potassium
0.2g Total Carbohydrates

0.1g Dietary Fiber
0g Sugars 41g Protein

CHICKEN RECIPES

CHESAPEAKE GARLIC PARMESAN WINGS

Prep Time: 15 Minutes
Cooking Time: 1 Hour & 35 Minutes
Servings: 6 Persons

Ingredients:
For Wings
2 to 4 pounds' chicken wings
Pepper & salt to taste
For Garlic Parmesan Sauce
1 cup hot sauce, any of your favorite
2 tablespoons parmesan, grated
1 stick of butter
2 tablespoons minced garlic
1 teaspoon old bay seasoning
¼ cup raw honey

Directions:
1. Preheat your pellet grill at 350 F earlier.

2. Cook the bird wings till an inner temperature displays one hundred 45 F.

3. In the meantime, put together the sauce. Next, over mild warmness in a big sauce pan; warmness the complete sauce substances collectively. Slowly upload the butter & deliver the elements a great stir until the butter is melted completely. Continue to stir the ingredient till the sauce elements and butter are mixed calmly; set the aggregate aside.

4. Prepare a Dutch oven with oil for frying. Heat the oil until very hot.

5. five. Remove the hen pieces from smoker & positioned the hen into the fry basket. Fry the bird for more than one minutes, till they reflect internal temperature of a hundred sixty-five F.

6. Place the cooked wings on a baking sheet lined with paper towel & maintain to cook for 5 to 10 extra mins.

7. Toss the wings with organized sauce till protected completely.

8. Serve hot and enjoy.

Nutrition Value (per serving)
1035 Calories
712 Calories from Fat
79g Total Fat
35g Saturated Fat
1.5g Trans Fat
11g Polyunsaturated Fat
27g Monounsaturated Fat
249mg Cholesterol
2785mg Sodium
513mg Potassium
43g Total Carbohydrates
1.3g Dietary Fiber
19g Sugars 40g Protein

GRILLED CHICKEN DRUMSTICKS WITH SAVORY CARAMEL

Ingredients:
Vegetable oil (for the grill)
4 grated garlic cloves
1 grated lemongrass stalk
½ cup sugar
¼ cup unseasoned rice vinegar
2 tsp crushed red pepper flakes
2 tsp grounded cumin
1 tsp grounded black pepper
3 tbsp. fish sauce
12 large chicken drumsticks (about 3 lb.)
Kosher salt

Directions:
1. Set up the grill for pinnacle indirect heat. Add the garlic, lemongrass, sugar, the vinegar, crimson pepper flakes, cumin, the black pepper, and ½ cup water to boil in a small pan, stirring occasionally and cook until reduced to ½ cup, about eight minutes. Let it cool and add inside the fish sauce. Move half of the sauce to a tiny bowl and positioned aside for serving.

2. Season the chicken with salt. Put the hen over oblique warmness. Grill, turning once or twice, till the pores and skin is singed and crisp and meat is cooked through, approximately 25–30 minutes. Move the hen to the hotter part of the grill and maintain grilling, turning frequently and spooning with the final sauce, until covered and lightly burned in places, 6 to 8 minutes longer. Serve with reserved sauce.

PINEAPPLE HABANERO WINGS

Prep Time: 20 Minutes
Cooking Time: 55 Minutes
Servings: 6 Persons

Ingredients:
For Wings
2-4 pounds' chicken wings
Juice of 2 limes, freshly squeezed Jamaican flavored rub
For The Pineapple Habanero Sauce
½ cup brown sugar

3 garlic cloves, minced

1 pineapple, cut into spears & grilled until grill marks appear

½ yellow pepper, diced

1 habanero, seeded & diced

1/3 cup white vinegar

2 tablespoons softened butter

Salt to taste

Directions:

For Wings

1. Drizzle the lime juice over the bird wings; make sure that they're nicely covered & then, generously season them with the Jamaican rub; set apart and allow them to marinate for overnight.

For Habanero Sauce

2. Blend the whole elements collectively in a food processor or blender (don't uploads the butter). Pour the organized mixture right into a sauce pan with the softened butter & let simmer on medium warmness for 10 to 15 mins.

3. Preheat your pellet smoker in advance to 225 F.

4. three. Smoke the wings for 40 to 45 mins; cautiously flip & growth the temperature to 350 F.

5. Cook them till they reflect an inner temperature of somewhere one hundred seventy-five to 180 F.

6. Remove the pieces from pellet grill & observe the organized sauce on each wing.

7. Increase your pellet grill's temperature to 450 F and put the portions on the grill again; prepare dinner until the sauce is set, for 5 to 7 extra mins. Serve warm and enjoy.

Nutrition Value (per serving)
919 Calories

549 Calories from Fat
61g Total Fat
23g Saturated Fat
0.8g Trans Fat
10g Polyunsaturated Fat
22g Monounsaturated Fat
201mg Cholesterol
946mg Sodium
560mg Potassium
53g Total Carbohydrates
1.9g Dietary Fiber
27g Sugars 39g Protein

SPICY GRILLED CHICKEN WITH CRUNCHY FENNEL SALAD

Ingredients:

Chicken

1½ lb. skinless, boneless chicken thighs

Kosher salt

2 garlic cloves

3 oil-packed anchovy fillets (optional)

1 red chili (Fresno or Holland), seeds removed and coarsely chopped

2 tbsps. of tomato paste

2 tsp finely chopped oregano

3 tbsps. of extra virgin olive oil, plus more for the grilling

2 halved lemons

Fennel Salad and Assembly

2 medium fennel bulbs, outer layers removed, halved lengthwise and thinly sliced

1 small white onion, thinly sliced into rounds

2 tbsps. unseasoned rice vinegar

2 tbsp. of extra virgin olive oil Kosher salt

1 tbsp. toasted sesame seeds

Directions:

Chicken

1. Pat the hen dry and season with salt, then put apart.

2. Smash the garlic the use of a knife on a cutting board. Add the anchovies, if the usage of, the chili and one or two of pinches of salt and hold mashing together with your knife till paste forms. (You may do this with a mortar and pestle.) Transfer the paste into a large bowl and add in the oregano and three tbsp. of oil. Add the hen and permit it take a seat for at least one hour.

3. Set up the grill for medium warmness. Clean and oil the grate. Grill the hen, turning once, till lightly burned and cooked through, about four minutes for every facet.

4. In the meantime, grill the lemons, cut side down, until gently burned and beginning to caramelize- approximately 4 mins. Move onto a platter.

5. Put the fowl onto the platter with lemons and let it rest for five mins.

Fennel dish and Assembly

1. While the chook is resting, toss the fennel, onion, and vinegar in a medium bowl, drizzle with oil and season with salt.

2. Place the fennel salad at the dish subsequent to the chicken and sprinkle with sesame seeds. Squeeze the grilled lemons over the bird and fennel salad.

GRILLED CHICKEN WITH BANANA PEPPERS

Ingredients:

2 finely grated garlic cloves
2 tbsp. of fresh lime juice 1 tbsp. fish sauce
1 tbsp. of cayenne pepper
1 tbsp. dark brown sugar
1 tbsp. garlic powder
2 tsp crushed red pepper flakes
2 tsp dried thyme
2 tsp ground allspice
2 tsp of onion powder
1 tsp grounded black pepper
1 tsp paprika
½ tsp ground cinnamon
½ tsp. of ground nutmeg
3 tbsp. vegetable oil and more for the grill
16 skin on, bone-in, chicken thighs (about 5½ lb.) Kosher salt
16 banana pepper thinly sliced lime wedges and chopped cilantro

Directions:

1. Put the garlic, lime juice, fish sauce, the cayenne, sugar, the garlic powder, purple pepper flakes, the dried thyme, the grounded allspice, onion powder, black pepper, the paprika, cinnamon, nutmeg and 3 tbsp. of oil in a huge bowl. Add the chook and season with salt. Let it sit down, turning chicken thighs once, for at the least two hours or kick back for one day.

2. Set up the grill for medium-high and indirect warmness and oil the grate. Put the chicken thighs, pores and skin side down, on the grate over the hottest a part of the grill and grill them, turning as soon as, till lightly burned, approximately 5 to 10 minutes. Move the fowl onto the cooler a part of the grill and preserve grilling, turning many times, till the instant-study thermometer inserted into the thickest element registers 165°, greater or less 20–25 minutes longer. Place the fowl onto a platter and allow it rest for ten minutes.

3. Top it with the banana peppers and

cilantro and serve with lime wedges.

HONEY MUSTARD GRILLED CHICKEN THIGHS

Ingredients:
45 boneless, skinless chicken thighs Glaze
34 tbsp. of honey
1/4 cup Dijon mustard
2 tbsp. of olive oil
1 tsp garlic powder
1 tsp Kosher salt
1 tsp grounded pepper

Directions:
1. In a small bowl, add the mustard, the honey, the olive oil and garlic powder, and blend for about 2 mins.
2. Put the bird thighs right into a resalable plastic bag and add the marinade, then season with salt and grounded pepper. Put inside the fridge for as a minimum 30 minutes.
3. Set up the grill for medium-high heat.
4. Put the bird thighs on the grill, cook dinner 3 or 5 minutes for each aspect, or until chicken is well roasted. Brush the bird with the remaining marinade on every facet even as grilling for the alternative 1 or 2 mins. When the hen is nicely cooked through, take it off the grill and serve even as nonetheless warm.

APRICOT CHIPOTLE CHICKEN THIGHS

Prep Time: 20 Minutes
Cooking Time: 1 Hour & 20 Minutes
Servings: 8 Persons

Ingredients:
3 to 4 pounds' bone-in chicken thighs
1 teaspoon smoked paprika
Apricot preserves, preferably 12 ounce
¼ cup BBQ sauce
1 teaspoon garlic powder
2-3 tablespoons chipotle peppers (diced) in adobo sauce
¼ cup chicken broth
1 tablespoon chipotle seasoning
2 tablespoons Dijon mustard
¼ teaspoon salt

Directions:
1. Add the apricot preserves observed through garlic powder, smoked paprika, Dijon mustard, chicken broth, BBQ sauce, mango chipotle seasoning, chipotle peppers and salt in a medium-sized blending bowl; supply the elements an awesome stir for multiple mins, till combined well. Set approximately ½ cup aside for later use.
2. Place the bird thighs into a freezer bag; add the prepared apricot chipotle marinade; seal the bag & cowl the chook pieces evenly with the organized marinade.
3. Let marinade for more than one hours.
4. Preheat your pellet grill to 400 F in advance.
5. Carefully place the lined hen portions over the new grill, pores and skin facet down first & grill until the grill marks start to appear, for 10 mins. Flip the chook portions & continue to grill until an inner temperature displays 165 F.
6. Remove the pieces from grill & brush them with the kept-aside glaze aggregate. Serve hot & enjoy.

Nutrition Value (per serving)

574 Calories
302 Calories from Fat
34g Total Fat
9.1g Saturated Fat
0.2g Trans Fat
7.3g Polyunsaturated Fat
14g Monounsaturated Fat
216mg Cholesterol
660mg Sodium
525mg Potassium
32g Total Carbohydrates
0.6g Dietary Fiber
22g Sugars 38g Protein

TURKEY RECIPES

SMOKED TURKEY

Prep Time: 20 Minutes
Cooking Time: 1 Hour & 55 Minutes
Servings: 10 Persons

Ingredients:
1 whole turkey
½ lemon, medium-sized
Poultry rub, any of your favorite to coat
1 stick of softened butter, at room temperature
½ cup of white wine, chicken broth or liquid of choice
2 tablespoons each of pepper & salt
Directions:
1. Preheat your pellet grill over high smoke in advance.
2. Remove the neck and giblets from the turkey then, rinse under water; pat it dry the use of paper towels.

3. Next, combine the butter with pepper and salt in a small-sized mixing bowl.
4. Gently separate the pores and skin from legs and breast using your hands (make certain that you hold it attached & in a single piece).
5. Pour & evenly spread the prepared butter combination under the skin. Season the turkey with the poultry seasoning (at the outer part).
6. Fill the Turkey Cannon Infusion Roaster with approximately lemon & ½ cup of liquid. Next, smoke the turkey on high smoke for an hour. Set the temperature of your pellet grill to 350 F & continue to prepare dinner the turkey until the internal temperature of the meat displays a hundred and sixty F. Set aside & let relaxation more or less for 1/2 an hour.
7. Serve and enjoy.

Nutrition Value (per serving)
873 Calories
359 Calories from Fat
40g Total Fat
14g Saturated Fat
0.7g Trans Fat
8.3g Polyunsaturated Fat
12g Monounsaturated Fat
416mg Cholesterol 1990mg Sodium
1253mg Potassium
2.2g Total Carbohydrates
0.4g Dietary Fiber
0.6g Sugars 50g Protein

SPATCHCOCK TURKEY

Prep Time: 20 Minutes
Cooking Time: 1 Hour & 20 Minutes
Servings: 12 Persons

Ingredients:

For The Turkey
1 whole turkey (roughly 15 pounds), thawed
Salt to taste

For Turkey Stock Ingredients
4 carrots, sliced
1 onion, chopped
5 springs fresh thyme
1-quart unsalted chicken stock
5 springs fresh sage
1-quart water
4 stalks of celery, chopped

Directions:

1. Remove the giblet packet and neck from inside the turkey; set aside.
2. Cut out the back bone using kitchen shears or a sharp knife & set aside.
3. three. Lay the turkey flat, on a metallic rack & generously practice the dry brine on both sides (salt). Place in a refrigerator for in a single day to air dry.
4. Next, put the whole elements for turkey inventory in a large-sized roasting pan. Place the roasting pan over the pellet grill & placed the top shelf in its place (putting the turkey over the top shelf).
5. Grill the turkey until the inner temperature displays a hundred and sixty F, at 350 F.
6. Strain the turkey stock & sense free to apply it in gravy. Serve warm and enjoy.

Nutrition Value (per serving)
837 Calories
290 Calories from Fat
32g Total Fat
8.4g Saturated Fat
0.3g Trans Fat
8.4g Polyunsaturated Fat
10g Monounsaturated Fat
413mg Cholesterol 686mg Sodium
1417mg Potassium
4.8g Total Carbohydrates
1.1g Dietary Fiber
2.3g Sugars 125g Protein

TEQUILA LIME ROASTED TURKEY

Prep Time: 25 Minutes
Cooking Time: 2 Hours & 35 Minutes
Servings: 12 Persons

Ingredients:

9 garlic cloves
1 bone-in whole turkey (roughly 15 pounds), thawed
3 jalape ño chiles, cut in half & seeded
1 ¼ cups gold tequila
3 ounces' olive oil
1 ½ teaspoons pepper
3 limes, cut into wedges
1 ¼ cups lime juice, fresh
¾ cups each of orange juice & chicken broth
3 tablespoon chili powder
1 tablespoon salt

Directions:

1. Preheat your smoker to 325 F in advance. Place the turkey breast in a shallow roasting pan, preferably pores and skin aspect up.
2. Place the jalapeno & garlic in a mini meals processor. Cover & process on high strength until chopped finely. Add the chili powder observed by using three oz. of tequila, three oz. of lime juice, oil, pepper and salt. Cover & method on high electricity again till the aggregate is

completely smooth.

3. Next, the usage of spoon or fingers; loosen the turkey pores and skin & rub the organized garlic aggregate over and underneath the turkey pores and skin; calmly pour the leftover blend on top of the turkey. Insert an ovenproof meat thermometer into the thickest part of the breast & make certain that it doesn't't touch the bone.

4. Pour the broth and orange juice observed by using the leftover lime juice and tequila into a roasting pan.

5. Roast until the thermometer displays an analyzing of one hundred 65 F, uncovered.

6. Place the turkey on a warm platter and then, cover with aluminum foil. Let stand for 12 to 15 minutes before carving. Spoon the pan juices on pinnacle of the turkey & garnish your dish with some clean lime wedges. Enjoy.

Nutrition Value (per serving)
517 Calories
341 Calories from Fat
38g Total Fat
17g Saturated Fat
1.8g Polyunsaturated Fat
18g Monounsaturated Fat
154mg Cholesterol
118mg Sodium
558mg Potassium
0.3g Total Carbohydrates
0g Dietary Fiber
0g Sugars 44g Protein

FISH RECIPES

JAPANESE SMOKED SALMON

Prep Time: 20 Minutes
Cooking Time: 1 Hour & 10 Minutes
Servings: 6 Persons

Ingredients:
2 salmon, fillets (skin removed)
1 teaspoon black pepper
3 cedar plank, untreated
1 teaspoon garlic, minced
1/3 cup soy sauce
1 teaspoon fresh parsley, minced
1/3 cup olive oil
1 teaspoon sesame oil
1 ½ tablespoons r ice vinegar
1 teaspoon onion, salt

Directions:
1. 1. For Japanese Salmon Marinade: Combine olive oil with sesame oil, rice vinegar, minced garlic, and soy sauce in a large-sized blending bowl till frivolously mixed. Add the salmon fillets; turning the piece's numerous times until first-class covered & let marinate for an hour, at room temperature.

2. Soak the cedar planks for an hour or two in heat water.

3. Preheat your grill on smoke with the lid open for multiple mins, till you could see a fireplace inside the burn pot. Preheat it to 225 F earlier. Once done; place the cedar planks on the grate and wait till the forums crackle a bit & start to smoke.

4. Remove the fish from marinade and then, generously season it with the parsley, onion powder & black pepper; discard any extra marinade. Carefully place the lined salmon over the planks & grill for 25 to 30 minutes, till the internal temperature reads 140 F.

5. Remove from the grill & let relaxation for a couple of mins; serve warm & enjoy.

Nutrition Value (per serving)
180 Calories
149 Calories from Fat
17g Total Fat
2.6g Saturated Fat
0g Trans Fat
2.7g Polyunsaturated Fat
10g Monounsaturated Fat
16mg Cholesterol
788mg Sodium
172mg Potassium
1.1g Total Carbohydrates
0.2g Dietary Fiber
0.1g Sugars 7g Protein

GRILLED SALMON

Prep Time: 20 Minutes
Cooking Time: 20 Minutes
Servings: 4 Persons

Ingredients:
4 (6 to 8 ounces) salmon fillets (with skin), remove the pin bones
Extra-virgin olive oil
½ lemon, cut into 4 wedges
Freshly ground black pepper & kosher salt to taste
Directions:
1. Preheat your grill over medium-

excessive heat (approximately four hundred to 450 F), for direct cooking. When the grill is nearly 350 F, location the solid iron skillet or griddle inside the center of your grill & let it get warm as properly.

2. Pat dry the salmon the use of paper towels and then, generously brush the pieces with oil & then, season with pepper and salt, ideally the flesh facet.

3. Carefully, vicinity the coated fillets without delay over the new griddle the usage of a steel spatula, flesh facet down first. It's important that allows you to flippantly space the fillets. Close the lid & allow the fillets to sear for more than one minutes, until they don't stick and you may easily raise them off the griddle, over direct medium-excessive warmth.

4. Carefully turn over the fillets; near the lid & preserve cooking for three to five more mins, till you get your favored doneness. Slip a spatula between the flesh and pores and skin then, switch the cooked fillets to warmed, person serving plates. Serve right now with some fresh lemon wedges on side and enjoy.

Nutrition Value (per serving)
211 Calories
133 Calories from Fat
15g Total Fat
3.1g Saturated Fat
0g Trans Fat
3.7g Polyunsaturated Fat
5.7g Monounsaturated Fat
47mg Cholesterol
196mg Sodium
331mg Potassium
1.3g Total Carbohydrates
0.4g Dietary Fiber

GRILLED SALMON STEAKS WITH CILANTRO AND GARLIC YOGURT SAUCE

Ingredients:
vegetable oil (for the grill)
2 serrano chiles
2 garlic cloves
1 cup cilantro leaves
½ cup plain whole-milk Greek yogurt
1 tbsp. of extra virgin olive oil
1 tsp honey
Kosher salt
2 12 oz. bone-in salmon steaks

Directions:
Set up the grill for medium-excessive heat, then oil the grate. Expel and dispose of seeds from one chili. Mix the 2 chiles, garlic, cilantro, the yogurt, oil, the nectar, and ¼ cup water in a blender until it turns into smooth, then season properly with salt.

Move 1/2 of the sauce to a touch bowl and put it aside. Season the salmon steaks with salt. Grill it, turning more than once, till it's beginning to turn dark, approximately 4 mins. Keep on grilling, turning frequently, and seasoning with residual sauce for as a minimum four minutes longer. Present with the stored sauce nearby.

GRILLED FRESH FISH

Prep Time: 10 Minutes
Cooking Time: 25 Minutes
Servings: 4 Persons

Ingredients:

1 whole firm white fish fillet: such as halibut, sea bass or cod
2 whole lemons; sliced into half
Traeger Fin & Feather Rub, as required

Directions:
1. Preheat your wood pellet to 325 F in advance for 12 to 15 mins, lid closed.
2. Season the fish with Rub & let take a seat for half an hour.
3. Place the fish & lemons without delay over the hot grill grates, cut facet down. Cook till the fish is flaky, for 12 to 15 mins. Ensure that you don't over cook dinner the fish. Serve right now with grilled lemons and enjoy.

GRILLED FISH WITH SALSA VERDE

Ingredients:
2 garlic cloves
3 tbsp. fresh orange juice
1 tsp dried oregano
2 cups of chopped white onion
¾ cup chopped cilantro
¼ cup extra virgin olive oil and more for the grill
5 tbsp. fresh lime juice
1 lb. of tilapia, striped bass or sturgeon fillets
Kosher salt and grounded pepper
1 cup of mayonnaise
1 tbsps. of milk
4 corn tortillas
2 avocados, peeled and sliced
½ small head of cabbage, cored and thinly sliced
Salsa Verde lime wedges

Directions:
1. Mix the garlic, orange juice, oregano,

one cup onion, ¼ cup cilantro, ¼ cup oil, and three tbsp. of lime juice in a medium bowl. Season the fish with salt and level-headed pepper. Spoon the 1/2 onion combination on a glass baking dish then put the fish on it. Spoon the closing onion combination over the fish and chill for half of hour. Turn the fish, cover and chill for another 1/2 hour.

2. Mix the mayo, milk, and the final two tbsp. of lime juice in a little bowl.

3. Set up the grill for medium-high warmth and brush the grate with oil. Grill the fish, with a few marinade on, until opaque inside the center, approximately 3–five mins for each aspect. Grill the tortillas until slightly burned, about ten seconds per facet.

4. Coarsely chop the fish and positioned it onto a platter. Serve with lime mayonnaise, tortillas, avocados, cabbage, Salsa Verde, lime wedges and the remaining cup of sliced onion and ½ cup cilantro.

SEAFOOD RECIPES

GRILLED TEXAS SPICY SHRIMP

Prep Time: 20 Minutes
Cooking Time: 20 Minutes
Servings: 8 Persons

Ingredients:
2 pounds' jumbo shrimp, peeled & deveined; washed; drain & pat dry
1 whole jalape ño pepper, seeded and minced
2 garlic clove, minced
½ cup fresh cilantro, finely chopped
1 small onion, finely diced
3 plus 1 tablespoon olive oil
1 cup BBQ Sauce
Ground black pepper & salt to taste

Directions:
1. Transfer the easy shrimp to a huge-sized blending bowl.

2. Gently blend with 2 tablespoons of oil and then, generously season with pepper and salt to taste; set aside until geared up to use.

3. For Sauce: Over medium-low heat in a large saucepan; warmness 1 tablespoon of olive oil till hot. Once done; add the jalape ño pepper, onion and garlic; sauté é for multiple mins, till turn softened and then, stir inside the barbeque sauce.

4. four. When you are equipped to cook the shrimp, preheat your wood pellet to 450 F, closed lid.

5. Carefully arrange the shrimp pieces over the new grill grate & cook dinner until the shrimp is corporation, opaque & cooked through, for 2 to three minutes on each side.

6. Quickly switch the cooked shrimp in conjunction with the freshly chopped cilantro into the nice and cozy sauce. Gently stir the ingredients until well coated; serve & enjoy.

Nutrition Value (per serving)
162 Calories
28 Calories from Fat
3.1g Total Fat
0.6g Saturated Fat
0g Trans Fat

0.6g Polyunsaturated Fat
1.5g Monounsaturated Fat
143mg Cholesterol
1006mg Sodium
235mg Potassium
17g Total Carbohydrates
0.6g Dietary Fiber
12g Sugars 16g Protein

BACON WRAPPED SCALLOPS

Prep Time: 20 Minutes
Cooking Time: 20 Minutes
Servings: 8 Persons

Ingredients:
½ pound bacon
1-pound sea scallops, large; dry using paper towels Sea salt to taste

Directions:
1. Preheat your pellet grill in step with the instructions to 350 F in advance.
2. Wrap the scallops in a cut piece of bacon & secure every piece using a toothpick.
3. Lay the scallops over the new grill, bacon-side-down. Close the lid & cook dinner for 5 to 7 minutes then, cautiously rotate the portions.
4. Continue to cook frivolously cooked on all sides. Serve hot & enjoy.

Nutrition Value (per serving)
157 Calories
104 Calories from Fat
12g Total Fat
3.8g Saturated Fat
0g Trans Fat
1.9g Polyunsaturated Fat
5g Monounsaturated Fat

32mg Cholesterol
483mg Sodium
172mg Potassium
2.2g Total Carbohydrates
0g Dietary Fiber
0.3g Sugars 10g Protein

VERACRUZ SCALLOPS WITH GREEN CHILE SAUCE

Prep Time: 20 Minutes
Cooking Time: 20 Minutes
Servings: 8 Persons

Ingredients:
24 (2 ounces) sea scallops, large pieces
Finely grated juice and zest of 1 lime, fresh
Vegetable oil, as required
For Rub
1 teaspoon pure chili powder
½ teaspoon ground cumin
1 teaspoon paprika
½ teaspoon oregano, dried
1 teaspoon kosher salt
¼ teaspoon freshly ground black pepper
For Sauce
3 long Anaheim chili peppers
½ cup sour cream
3 scallions (green and white parts only), coarsely chopped
½ cup mayonnaise
1 garlic clove, small
¼ cup fresh cilantro leaves & tender stems; loosely packed
Finely grated juice & zest of 1 lime, fresh
¼ teaspoon kosher salt
Directions:
1. Preheat the grill over high heat for direct cooking.

2. Grill the chili peppers for multiple mins, until turn blackened & blistered in spots, with the lid open, turning every now and then. Remove the chiles from grill; set aside till clean to handle. Once done; put off the stem ends & discard. Scrape off & discard the blackened skins using a pointy knife. Coarsely chop the leftover parts of chiles & drop them into a blender or meals processor. Add the scallions followed by using garlic, and cilantro. Process on excessive strength until you get coarse paste like consistency; scraping down the edges of your bowl as required. Add the leftover sauce ingredients & technique on high electricity again till you get smooth sauce.
3. Next, mix the entire rub ingredients together in a small-sized mixing bowl.
4. four. Rinse the scallops underneath cold jogging tap water & take away the tough, small muscle. Place the cleaned scallops in a large-sized blending bowl & upload oil (sufficient to coat). Add the rub aggregate followed by way of the lime juice, and lime zest. Mix well until the scallops are flippantly coated.
5. Grill the scallops for 4 to six mins, until opaque inside the center and organization slightly at the surface, with the lid closed, turning once. Remove from the grill; serve heat with the prepared sauce and enjoy.

Nutrition Value (per serving)
208 Calories
182 Calories from Fat
20g Total Fat
4.3g Saturated Fat
0.3g Trans Fat
10g Polyunsaturated Fat
4.6g Monounsaturated Fat

22mg Cholesterol 698mg Sodium
168mg Potassium
5g Total Carbohydrates
0.9g Dietary Fiber
2.3g Sugars 2.4g Protein

VEGETABLES RECIPES

HERB ROASTED POTATOES

Prep Time: 20 Minutes
Cooking Time: 1 Hour & 20 Minutes
Servings: 8 Persons

Ingredients:
4 pounds' yellow potatoes, cubed into small, pieces; preferably bite-sized
2 tablespoons fresh rosemary, chopped
6 garlic cloves, minced
2 tablespoons fresh thyme, chopped
3 tablespoons olive oil
2 tablespoons fresh sage, chopped
Salt and pepper to taste
Directions:
1. Preheat your pellet grill to 375 F in advance.
2. Cube the potatoes & blend them with garlic, oil and herbs. Spread a thin layer of coated potatoes in a skillet (preferably cast iron) & roast for an hour, till turn golden brown, soft & crispy. Stirring the potatoes once in the course of the roasting process; serve hot & enjoy.

Nutrition Value (per serving)
224 Calories
48 Calories from Fat

5.3g Total Fat
0.8g Saturated Fat
0g Trans Fat
0.6g Polyunsaturated Fat
3.7g Monounsaturated Fat
0mg Cholesterol
14mg Sodium
981mg Potassium
41g Total Carbohydrates
5g Dietary Fiber
1.9g Sugars 4.9g Protein

GRILLED HALIBUT NICOISE WITH MARKET VEGETABLES

Ingredients:
4 large eggs
1½ pounds skin on halibut fillets
2 tbsp. plus ¼ cup olive oil
Kosher salt and grounded pepper
2 pounds of mixed vegetables (scallions, garlic scrapes, Romano beans, halved small eggplants, halved new potatoes)
4 cups torn lettuce leaves
1 cup of halved Sun Gold tomatoes
1 bunch of trimmed and halved small breakfast radishes
1 cup of Green Olive Tapenade

Directions:
1. Boil the eggs in a massive pot of effervescent water for 7 minutes. Drain and flow in a large bowl of ice water, then allow them to cool.
2. Set up the grill for medium-excessive warmth. Spoon the halibut with 2 tbsp. of oil and season with salt and grounded pepper. Grill, pores and skin side down, until it's miles singed and fish is cooked through- about 5 to 8 mins. Turn and grill for another minute. Move halibut onto a plate and take off the skin.
3. Mix the veggies with ¼ cup oil in a big bowl and season with salt and down to earth pepper. Grill them, turning as soon as in a while, till gently singed and tender. Time could be extraordinary for each vegetable (around 2 minutes for scallions and garlic scrapes, four minutes for Romano beans, eight–10 minutes for eggplants, 10–15 for potatoes). Move onto a plate as they're finished.
4. Cautiously strip and cut the eggs. Place lettuce leaves on a platter and upload the halibut, the grilled greens, tomatoes, radishes and eggs on pinnacle.
5. Spoon some Green Olive Tapenade over and serve.

GRILLED GREENS AND CHEESE QUESADILLAS

Ingredients:
2 tbsp. vegetable oil
½ medium white onion, finely chopped
2 finely grated garlic cloves
10 ounces' Swiss chard or chopped nettle
2 tsp of fresh lime juice
Kosher salt
6 ounces Toma cheese or grated sharp cheddar
8 corn tortillas
Grilled Salsa Roja
Avocado
Tomatillo
Salsa Verde

Directions:
1. Heat the oil in a big skillet. Cook the onion and garlic, turning as soon as in a while, for approximately 6 or 8 minutes.

Add the greens, a group at a time. Pour in ½ cup water and cook, every now and then turning, until greens are delicate, for approximately 6 or 8 minutes. Add the lime juice then season with salt. Move onto a plate and let it cool.

2. Heat a skillet over medium heat and upload 2 tbsp. of cheddar proper on it. Top with a tortilla and cook, squeezing with a spatula, until cheddar is softened and crisp, around 1 minute. Put the cheddar facet up on a baking sheet. Repeat with the other cheese and tortillas to make 7 extra quesadillas. Top every quesadilla with 2 tbsp. of veggies combination, fold them in half, and keep cooking, turning once, till the vegetables are heat and tortillas are toasted- around four minutes.

3. Serve the quesadillas with Grilled Salsa Roja and Avocado Tomatillo Salsa Verde.

GRILLED CORN ON THE COB

Prep Time: 20 Minutes
Cooking Time: 30 Minutes
Servings: 2 Persons

Ingredients:
Corn on the cob, fresh
Butter & salt for serving
Directions:
1. Preheat your pellet grill over excessive warmth in advance.

2. Remove some outer layers of the corn husks.

3. Remove the top from every cob using scissors & trim any free husk leaves as well. Place the corn over the new grill (preferably in their husks) & close the lid.

Cook for 25 to 30 minutes, till all sides of the husks flip charred, turning after each eight to 10 mins.

4. Remove the corn from grill. Let take a seat till you can easily cope with it, for a couple of minutes. Remove the charred husks & silks from the corn.

5. Apply some butter and salt on hot corn; rubbing it nicely. Serve warm and enjoy.

Nutrition Value (per serving)
90 Calories
6.3 Calories from Fat
0.7g Total Fat
0.2g Saturated Fat
0g Trans Fat
0.2g Polyunsaturated Fat
0.1g Monounsaturated Fat
0.9mg Cholesterol
52mg Sodium
291mg Potassium
19g Total Carbohydrates
3.2g Dietary Fiber
2.3g Sugars 3.6g Protein

GRILLED CITRUS SHRIMP LETTUCE CUPS

Ingredients:
1 small finely chopped shallot
1 5inch lemongrass stalk, outer layers removed and finely chopped
1 thinly sliced Thai chili
½ cup fresh lime juice
½ cup fresh orange juice
2 tsp of finely chopped peeled ginger
1 tsp (or more) Kosher salt
1 pound of peeled, deveined large shrimp, tails removed
2 tsp of toasted sesame oil cooked white

rice, Little Gem lettuce leaves, sliced cucumber or julienned carrot, lime wedges, mint sprigs, and toasted sesame seeds

Directions:

1. Mix the shallot, lemongrass, the chili, lime and orange juice, ginger, and salt in a little bowl. Cover and let it take a seat at room temperature. Pour some marinade over the shrimp in a medium bowl, cowl, and relax for 30 mins. Set up the grill for medium-excessive heat. Grill the shrimp till softly singed and cooked through, approximately 1–2 minutes for each facet. Move the shrimp right into a big bowl and blend with sesame oil, then season with salt.

2. Serve the shrimp with rice, lettuce, cucumber or carrots, lime wedges, mint, sesame seeds, and marinade for making lettuce cups.

GRILLED SQUID WITH CHILE DRESSING AND RADISHES

Ingredients:

Dressing

3 dried ancho chiles
2 dried chiles de árbol
1 dried pasilla chili
1 dried ají amarillo chili
2 Large or 4 small radishes
garlic cloves
2 tbsp. of sherry vinegar or red wine vinegar
1 tbsp. of fresh lemon juice
1 tsp of honey
½ tsp smoked paprika
Kosher salt and grounded pepper
½ cup of olive oil

Squid

2 pounds of cleaned large squid (bodies and tentacles separated)
5 finely grated garlic cloves
½ cup of mayonnaise
½ cup of red wine vinegar Kosher salt and grounded pepper
vegetable oil
1 tbsp. of fresh lemon juice

Salad and Assembly

⅓ cup parsley leaves
1 tbsp. thinly sliced chives 1 tbsp. of marjoram leaves
1 tbsp. lemon juice
Kosher salt and grounded pepper ½ cup torn Castelvetrano olives olive oil

Directions:

Dressing

1. Mix the ancho chiles, chiles de árbol, the pasilla chiles, and aji amarillo chili and cover with bubbling water. Cover with Saran wrap and let it relaxation for approximately 20–25 minutes. Drain.

2. Take off the seeds from chiles. Cut off the tops of radishes and chop them. Slice the radishes and positioned away for the salad. Mix the chiles, radish tops, garlic, the vinegar, lemon juice, the honey and paprika in a blender, then season with salt and grounded pepper. Mix until the chiles are finely chopped. Add the oil and blend until smooth.

Squid

1. Set up the grill for excessive warmness. Cover a large skillet with 2 layers of foil and set at the grate.

2. Taking one at a time, reduce the squid our bodies into triangles. Discard the cartilage. Using a knife scratch away the jellylike membrane lining the interior of

the body. Rinse the squid parts well and pat dry with paper towels.

3. Mix the garlic, mayonnaise, the vinegar, a bit of salt and pepper in a massive resalable plastic bag. Add the squid, seal the bag, squeezing out the air, and relax for 30 mins.

4. Oil the grate after cleansing it with a cord brush. Place more than one squid pieces at the grate and quickly cowl with the recent skillet. Grill till marks display up, around 45 seconds, then flip over. Set the skillet returned on pinnacle and grill until marks display up, about every other 45 seconds. Move the squid into a medium bowl. Repeat with the last squid.

5. Add lemon juice to the bowl with squid and season with extra salt, then pass onto a platter. Sprinkle with dressing.

<u>Salad and Assembly</u>

1. Mix the parsley, chives, the marjoram, lemon juice, and radishes in a medium bowl, then season with salt and grounded pepper. Spread the salad over the squid, top with olives, and sprinkle with oil.

SMOKED MASHED POTATOES

Prep Time: 20 Minutes
Cooking Time: 2 Hours & 20 Minutes
Servings: 4 Persons

Ingredients:
6 russet potatoes
1 cube butter, melted
2 sweet potatoes
1 cup sour cream
2 tablespoons chives, chopped
1-pint buttermilk

Garlic salt, pepper & salt to taste
Directions:
1. Preheat your pellet grill over Hi Smoke in advance. When done, area the entire potatoes over the recent grate.
2. Smoke the potatoes until flip fork tender, for two hours. Next, the usage of a hand mixer or fork; mash the potatoes. Add the butter followed with the aid of buttermilk, chives, bitter cream, garlic salt, pepper, and salt; mix nicely. Serve hot & enjoy.

Nutrition Value (per serving)
422 Calories
138 Calories from Fat
15g Total Fat
8.4g Saturated Fat
0.6g Trans Fat
0.7g Polyunsaturated Fat
3.7g Monounsaturated Fat
46mg Cholesterol
320mg Sodium
1419mg Potassium
62g Total Carbohydrates
4.9g Dietary Fiber
12g Sugars 11g Protein

OTHER RECIPES

GRILLED CAULIFLOWER STEAKS AND SCALLIONS

Ingredients:
1 large head cauliflower
6 tbsp. of vegetable oil and more for the grill
1 bunch of trimmed scallions

Kosher salt and grounded pepper
1 1inch piece of grated ginger
garlic clove
½ cup (packed) of fresh cilantro leaves
1 tbsp. fresh lime juice gochujang, toasted
sesame seeds, and sesame oil

Directions:

1. Take off the leaves and trim the
cauliflower, leaving the middle untouched.
Put the cauliflower, center facet down, on a
work surface. Beginning from the midline
of the cauliflower, slice it into four ½"
"steaks".
2. Set up the grill for medium-excessive
warmth and oil the grate. Sprinkle
cauliflower steaks, florets, and scallions
with four tbsp. of oil, then season with
salt and level-headed pepper. Grill the
scallions, turning from time to time till
burned in spots, round 2 mins. Grill the
cauliflower steaks until delicate and singed
in spots, about 8–10 mins for each facet.
3. Mix the ginger, garlic, the cilantro, lime
juice, and a pair of tbsp. of oil in a blender
until the dressing has the consistency
of yogurt and season with salt. Put the
cauliflower and scallions onto a platter.
Sprinkle with gochujang and sesame seeds
and shower with sesame oil. Serve with
cilantro sauce nearby.

GRILLED SCALLOPS WITH HONEYDEW AVOCADO SALSA

Ingredients:
Finely grated lime zest
2 tbsp. of fresh lime juice
1 tbsp. of extra virgin olive oil and more for
the drizzling

1 1/2 pounds' honeydew melon, rind
removed and cut into 1/4inch dice
1 has avocado, cut into 1/4inch
Dice salt and ground black pepper
2 pounds of large sea scallops

Directions:

1. Set up the grill. In a massive bowl, blend
the lime zest and juice with one tbsp. of
olive oil. Utilizing an elastic spatula,
delicately add inside the diced honeydew
melon and avocado. Season the salsa with
salt and floor darkish pepper. Sprinkle the
scallops with olive oil and season with
salt and dark pepper. Grill over medium
warmth, turning once till gently singed and
cooked through, round three to four mins
for each aspect. Move the scallops onto
plates, spoon the salsa close by, and serve.
2. Grilled Sea Scallops with Corn Salad.

GRILLED SHRIMP WITH OREGANO AND LEMON

Ingredients:
1/2 cup salted capers, rinsed, better if
soaked for one hour and drained
1/2 cup oregano leaves
1 minced garlic clove
3/4 cup extra virgin olive oil
tsp finely grated lemon zest3 tbsp. of
freshly squeezed lemon juice
grounded pepper
1/2 pounds' large shrimp, shelled and
deveined salt

Directions:

On a cutting board, finely chop the capers.
Mix it with the oregano leaves and garlic.
Move it right into a bowl and add in half
cup and 2 tbsp. of the olive oil, then the

lemon zest and juice. Season the sauce with grounded pepper. Set up the grill. In a big bowl, positioned the shrimp with 2 tbsp. of olive oil and season with salt and level-headed pepper. String the shrimp onto steel skewers and grill them over high warmness, turning once, till the shrimp are softly singed and cooked through, around three mins for each facet. Expel the shrimp from the skewers and move them onto a platter. Spoon the sauce on pinnacle and serve.

GRILLED SHRIMP WITH SHRIMP BUTTER

Ingredients:
6 tbsp. unsalted butter
1/2 cup finely chopped red onion
1 1/2 tsp crushed red pepper
1 tsp Malaysian shrimp paste 1 1/2 tsp lime juice salt
grounded black pepper
24 shelled and deveined large shrimp
6 wooden skewers (better if soaked in water for 30 minutes) torn mint leaves and assorted sprouts

Directions:
1. In a little skillet, liquefy three tbsp. of butter. Add the onion then cook over slight heat for about 3 minutes. Add inside the squashed pink pepper and shrimp paste and prepare dinner until fragrant, approximately 2 mins.
2. Add inside the lime juice and the ultimate 3 tbsp. of butter and season with salt. Keep the shrimp sauce warm.
3. Set up the grill. Season the shrimp with salt and pepper and string onto the skewers, no longer too tightly. Grill over

high warmness, turning as soon as till gently singed and cooked through, round four mins. Move onto a platter and spoon with shrimp sauce. Spread at the mint leaves and sprouts and serve.

GRILLED SERRANO SALSA VERDE

Ingredients:
6–8 serranos chiles
1 bunch basil
1 bunch cilantro
1 bunch parsley
1¼ cups extra virgin olive oil
½ cup sherry vinegar or red wine vinegar
2½ tsp Kosher salt
Special Equipment
Metal or bamboo skewer

Directions:
1. Set up the grill for medium-excessive heat. String the chiles onto the skewers and grill, frequently turning, till singed, around 6 minutes. Let cool and discard the stems.
2. In the meantime, gather leaves from basil, cilantro and parsley. (You should have around 2 cups of every herb.)
3. Mix the chiles, basil, the cilantro, and parsley in a blender. Add oil, vinegar, and salt and mix until a thick sauce forms.
4. Serve it with Salsa Verde on top.
5. Do Ahead: Sauce may be made one day ahead. Cover and chill. Bring to room temperature earlier than serving.

GRILLED SCALLOPS WITH LEMONY SALSA VERDE

Ingredients:

2 tbsp. of vegetable oil and more for the grill

12 large sea scallops, side muscle removed

Kosher salt and grounded black pepper

Lemony Salsa Verde

Directions:

1. Set up the grill for medium-high warmness, then oil the grate. Toss the scallops with 2 tbsp. of oil on a rimmed baking sheet and season with salt and pepper. Utilizing a fish spatula or your hands, region the scallops on the grill. Grill them, sometimes turning, until gently singed and cooked through, round 2 mins for every aspect. Serve the scallops with Lemony Salsa Verde.

GRILLED SPICED SNAPPER WITH MANGO AND RED ONION SALAD

Ingredients:

1 5lb or two 2½lb head-on whole fish (red snapper or black sea bass), cleaned

Kosher salt

⅓ cup chaat masala, vadouvan or tandoori spice

⅓ cup vegetable oil and more for the grill

1 ripe but firm mango, cut into irregular pieces

1 rinsed and thinly sliced small red onion

1 bunch cilantro, coarsely chopped

3 tbsp. fresh lime juice

extra virgin olive oil lime wedges

Directions:

1. Put the fish on a slicing board and pat dry with paper towels. Use a knife to make diagonal cuts along the body each 2" on the 2 sides, cutting right all the way down to the bones. Season the fish with salt.

Cover it with the spice aggregate as a way to cowl the complete fish, head to tail. Let it sit down at room temperature for 20 mins.

2. In the meantime, installation the grill for medium-excessive heat. Clean and oil the grate.

3. Shower the two sides of fish with ⅓ cup of vegetable oil to cowl it. Grill the fish undisturbed for 10 mins. Lift up barely from one edge to check whether the skin is puffed and gently singed and if it discharges from the grate. If no longer yet, wait for one more second after which strive as soon as greater. When it's far prepared, smoothly slide two large metal spatulas beneath and flip it over.

4. Grill the fish till the opposite side is gently singed, and skin is puffed, approximately eight to 12 minutes, depending on the scale of the fish. Place onto a platter.

5. Toss the mango, onion, cilantro, the lime juice, and salt in a medium bowl. Shower with a hint of olive oil and mix again, then cover. Spread the salad over the fish and gift it with lime wedges.

GRILLED BABY BACK RIBS WITH TAMARIND GLAZE

Ingredients:

Ribs

2 racks of halved baby back pork ribs (3½–4 pounds)

5 ounces' ginger, peeled and chopped

1 orange wedge (about ⅛ of orange)

5-star anise pods

2½ cups unfiltered apple juice

1 tbsp. Diamond Crystal or 2 tbsp. Kosher salt

6 habanero chiles, halved lengthwise, seeds removed if desired and divided

¼ cup plus ⅓ brown sugar

½ cup ketchup

⅓ cup apple cider vinegar

¼ cup tamarind concentrate

3 tbsp. of honey

<u>Salad and Assembly</u>

vegetable oil

Kosher salt

1 Persian cucumber, thinly sliced

½ thinly sliced small red onion

½ thinly sliced serrano chili

2 tsp fresh lime juice micro cilantro and lime wedges

Directions:

<u>Ribs</u>

1. Put the ribs in a Dutch oven or some other heavy pot. Then add the ginger, orange wedge, star anise, the apple juice, then salt, half of chiles, and ¼ cup brown sugar. Pour in as tons' water because it takes simply to cowl the beef and produce to a simmer over medium warmness. Reduce warmth at a completely mild simmer, partially cowl the pot and braise, turning the racks a few times, until the beef is fork-smooth and nearly falling off the bones, approximately 1½–2 hours. In the meantime, chop the remaining chiles and placed them aside.

2. Transfer the ribs onto a rimmed baking sheet and allow them to cool. Cut among ribs which will create 2 rib pieces

3. In the meantime, increase the heat underneath the Dutch oven to high

and add ketchup, vinegar, tamarind concentrate, then honey, the last ⅓ cup brown sugar, and reserved chopped chiles to broiling liquid. Cook it, often tossing, till the glaze is thick, extra or less 30–45 mins. Strain it into a big measuring cup so that it will discard solids. Let it settle so the oil rises to the surface. Pour off the oil right into a small bowl then set aside.

4. Do Ahead: Ribs can be grilled in the future ahead. Let them cool in liquid, then cowl and chill.

<u>Salad and Assembly</u>

1. Prepare the grill for medium warmness, then oil the grate. Taking one at a time, dip the ribs into the glaze. Grill the ribs, turning several times, till the glaze is lightly charred, approximately five minutes' total. Put the ribs onto a platter then season with salt. Drizzle with the ultimate glaze and oil.

2. Stir the cucumber, the onion, chili, and lime juice in a medium bowl to combine all then season with salt. Now unfold salad over the ribs and top with micro cilantro. To be served with lime wedges.

GRILLED RED MULLET WITH CHARRED ONIONS AND PINE NUTS

Ingredients:

¼ cup extra virgin olive oil and more for the grill

⅓ cup pine nuts

4 small unpeeled onions

¼ cup of drained capers

¼ cup of raisins

¼ cup red wine vinegar

Kosher salt

8 whole red mullets or 4 red snappers
1 cup parsley leaves
Aleppo style or red pepper flakes
and lemon wedges

Directions:

1. Set up the grill for medium-high warmth. Clean the grate nicely with a brush and then oil it. Toast the cracked pine nuts on a rimmed baking sheet, moving as soon as, till they become golden brown, about 5 mins, and permit cool. Grill the onions, turning once in a while, until skins are blackened and onions have softened, about 15–20 minutes. Put onto a platter and allow cool for ten mins.

2. Split the onions, remove the outer peel, and discard it. Separate the onion layers into character petals. Put into a medium bowl and upload in the cracked pine nuts, capers, the raisins and vinegar, then season with salt.

3. Season the fish with salt, drizzle with ¼ cup oil. Grill till the pores and skin is gently burned, and flesh is flaky and opaque to the bone, about 3 minutes for mullet and eight minutes for snapper. Using a steel spatula lightly flip it over onto the opposite side. Cook until the flesh is flaky and opaque, approximately three–8 minutes.

4. Move the fish onto a platter and spoon with vinaigrette, pinnacle with parsley and some red pepper flakes, then drizzle with oil. Serve with lemon wedges.

CHILE LIME CLAMS WITH TOMATOES AND GRILLED BREAD

Ingredients:

6 tbsp. unsalted pieces of butter
2 large shallots, chopped
4 thinly sliced garlic cloves
1 tbsp. of tomato paste 1 cup of beer
1 cup cherry tomatoes
1 15. 5 ounce can-chickpeas, rinsed
2 tbsp. sambal oleic
24 scrubbed littleneck clams
1 tbsp. fresh lime juice
4 thick slices of country-style bread
2 tbsp. olive oil
Kosher salt
½ cup cilantro leaves
lime wedges

Directions:

1. Set up the grill for medium, oblique warmth. Put a large skillet on the grill over direct warmness and melt 4 tbsp. of butter in it.

2. Add the shallots and garlic and keep cooking, frequently stirring, till they soften, about four mins. Add the tomato paste and keep cooking, continually stirring, till paste darkens to a wealthy brick red color. Add the beer and tomatoes.

3. Cook until the beer is reduced almost by half of, approximately four mins. Add within the chickpeas and sambal oleic, then the clams.

4. Cover and hold cooking till clams have opened, maybe from 5 to 10 mins relying on the scale of clams and the heat. Discard any clams that don't open. Pour inside the lime juice and the last 2 tbsp. of butter. While grilling the clams, you could sprinkle the bread with oil and season with salt. Grill till it will become golden brown and crisp, approximately 2 minutes for each side.

5. Put the toasts onto plates and spoon

HONEY GRILLED APRICOTS

Ingredients:
3 tbsp. of unsalted butter
2 tbsp. of sugar
6 to 8 halved apricots
2 tbsp. of honey
1 lemon (4 wedges)
Optional: ice cream or Brie cheese
1 tsp of cinnamon mint leaves

Directions:
1. Liquefy the butter and sugar together in a massive dish.
2. Add the apricots and coat with the butter aggregate.
3. Grill for six to 7 mins, turning frequently.
4. When cooked, positioned the apricots on dessert plates reduce facet up, shower with honey and lemon juice, and serve warm with a piece of ice cream or with cuts of Brie cheese.
5. Top with cinnamon and mint leaves.

GRILLED CARROTS WITH AVOCADO AND MINT

Ingredients:
1 tsp cumin seeds
3 tbsp. fresh lemon juice
2 tsp honey
¼ cup plus 2 tbsp. of extra virgin olive oil
1 thinly sliced serrano chili
1 1" piece ginger, peeled and finely grated
Kosher salt
1½ lb. medium carrots, scrubbed, halved lengthwise, tops trimmed to about 1"
2 avocados, cut into large pieces
½ cup mint leaves

Directions:
Set up the grill for medium warmness. Toast the cumin seeds in a dry little skillet over medium warmness, tossing regularly, till fragrant, round 2 mins. Let it cool. Rudely squash the cumin seeds in a mortar and pestle or with the flat aspect of a knife. Move into a giant bowl. Squeeze the lemon and add the honey. Add within the oil and as soon as consolidated, mix inside the chili and ginger. Season with salt and let it take a seat.

Hurl the carrots with 2 tbsp. of oil on a rimmed baking sheet and season with salt. Grill the carrots, turning as soon as in a while till delicately singed in spots, extra or less 14–18 minutes. Move the carrots into the bowl with sauce. Cover and season with salt.

Place the avocado and carrots onto a platter. Spoon away any additional sauce at that point top with mint. Serve carrots heat or at room temperature.

EASIEST EVER GRILLED VEGGIE BURGERS

Ingredients:
2 tbsp. of extra virgin olive oil and more for the grill
1 14oz block extra firm tofu, drained
2 14. 5oz cans black beans, rinsed and well-drained
¼ cup almond butter
¼ cup mayonnaise (vegan, if you are vegan)
2 finely grated garlic cloves
4 tsp chili powder
4 tsp. Diamond Crystal or 2 tsp Kosher salt
2 cups cooked quinoa
¼ cup flaxseed meal 2 tbsp. cornstarch

toasted buns, pickled onions,tomato,lettuce, pickles, and chipotle yogurt

Directions:

1. Set up the grill for medium-excessive and direct heat. Clean and oil the grate. Shred the tofu and firmly squeeze it in among paper towels to drain the maximum quantity excess liquid.

2. Heat a pair of tbsp. oil in a big pan over medium warmth. Cook the tofu and beans, often moving, till beans look barely dried out, and their skins location darkened-about 10 to 12 minutes.

3. Meanwhile, whisk almond butter and mayo in a medium bowl. Add inside the garlic, the chili powder, and the salt. Add tofu-bean mixture and the cornstarch and mix.

4. Add the flaxseed and ¼ cup of bloodless water in a touch bowl. Let it sit for about one minute. Put in the tofu-bean mixture and blend.

5. Using oiled hands, flip the combination into 8–10 patties concerning ½" thick. Grill them until lightly burned in spots, approximately a pair of minutes. Turn, using a metallic spatula and grill until lightly burned on the second side also and cooked through, approximately other 2 mins.

6. Place the burgers on the buns. Pile high with the onions, tomato, the lettuce, pickles, and chipotle yogurt. Put the other 1/2 of the bun on top and serve.

GRILLED APPLE AND BRIE FLATBREAD

Ingredients:
4 flatbread

4 flatbread
4 medium golden apples (cored and sliced)
6 to 7 ounces of Brie cheese
1/3 cup walnut (roughly chopped)
1/4 cup of honey
2 tbsp. of fresh thyme

Directions:

Recipe Preparation

1. Set up the grill for high warmth.

2. Put the apples on an oiled grate and cook for 2 to a few minutes for each side.

3. Take away from the warmth and permit cool for five mins.

4. Cut the apples into small slices and put aside.

5. Put the flatbread onto a big cutting board.

6. Sprinkle with olive oil.

7. Sprinkle thyme onto every piece and put the grilled apples and Brie cuts onto flatbread.

8. Put onto the grill and cook dinner for 5 mins or till the Brie starts to liquefy, and bread is pleasantly toasted.

9. Take far away from the heat, bathe with honey, and top with walnuts.

10. Cut into fourths and appreciate.

GRILLED PEAR AND SWEET POTATO SALAD

Ingredients:
2 peeled sweet potatoes cut into 1/2 inch pieces
1 large pear (peeled, cored and cut into 1/4 inch slices)
2 cups of baby arugula
2 cups of baby spinach
1/3 cup crumbled Feta cheese

1/4 cup of chopped toasted pecans
For the Dressing:
1/3 cup apple jelly
1/4 cup red wine vinegar
1 tbsp. of water
1 pinch of salt olive oil

Directions:

1. For the dressing, add the apple jelly, crimson wine vinegar, the water, and salt into a pot. Boil it, then decrease the warmth and permit stew till decreased to a syrupy consistency. Take far from the warmth and cool to room temperature.
2. Place the sweet potato cuts right into a massive pot with water and cook dinner for 1013 minutes. Pull out of the water, pat dry with paper towels and positioned them onto a baking sheet, cutting board or platter. Spoon with olive oil and season with salt.
3. Cautiously positioned the sweet potato and pear cuts onto the grill, and cook dinner for 34 mins for every side. When potatoes and pears have grill marks and a caramelized surface, eliminate from the warmth and circulate onto a clean baking sheet. Let them cool.
4. Place the salad onto a huge serving dish, top with candy potatoes and pears and crumbles of Feta cheese. Sprinkle cooled dressing onto the salad and top with pecans.

GRILLED CHICKEN WITH LEMON & CUMIN

Preparation Time: 3 hours and 15 minutes
Cooking Time: 10 minutes
Servings: 4

Ingredients:
4 chicken breast fillets
2 teaspoons olive oil
4 teaspoons ground cumin
2 tablespoons lemon juice
1 tablespoon lime juice
Salt and pepper to taste

Directions:
1. Coat the bird breast with oil.
2. In a bowl, blend the rest of the elements.
3. Brush the hen breast with the lemon and cumin aggregate.
4. Cover and marinate within the fridge for 3 hours.
5. Set your Traeger wood pellet grill to 350 degrees F.
6. Preheat for 15 minutes while the lid is closed.
7. Grill the chicken for five minutes in line with side.
8. Let relaxation for five minutes before serving.

Serving Suggestion: Serve with coleslaw. Preparation / Cooking Preparation / Cooking Tips: You can also pound the chook breast with a meat mallet earlier than getting ready it.

BARBECUE BACON BITES

Preparation Time: 10 minutes
Cooking Time: 30 minutes
Servings: 4

Ingredients:
1 tablespoon ground fennel
Salt and pepper to taste
1/2 cup brown sugar
1 lb. pork belly, sliced into cubes
Directions:
1. Preheat your Traeger timber pellet grill to 350 ranges F. For 15 minutes even as the lid is closed.
2. In a bowl, mix the ground fennel, salt, pepper and brown sugar.
3. Coat the bacon cubes with this mixture.
4. Grill for 30 minutes.
Serving Suggestion: Serve as appetizer.
Preparation / Cooking Tips: It's also a good concept to use a foil for cooking the bacon to seize the bacon drippings and reserve for later use.

GRILLED VENISON KEBAB

Preparation Time: 20 minutes
Cooking Time: 15 minutes
Servings: 4

Ingredients:
1 venison, sliced into cubes
2 red onions, sliced into wedges
2 red bell pepper, sliced into 2
2 yellow bell pepper, sliced into 2
Olive oil
Salt and pepper to taste
2 tablespoons lemon juice
1 1/2 tablespoons fresh mint leaves, chopped
1 1/2 tablespoons parsley, chopped
Directions:
1. Add the venison chunks, onion and bell peppers in a bowl.
2. Coat with olive oil and season with salt and pepper.
3. Thread onto skewers alternately.
4. In some other bowl, mix lemon juice, mint leaves and parsley. Set aside.
5. Set the Traeger wood pellet grill to excessive.
6. Preheat whilst the lid is closed for 10 minutes.
7. Grill the kebabs for 7 to eight minutes in line with side.
8. Brush with the lemon aggregate inside the closing minute of cooking.
Serving Suggestion: Serve with Greek yogurt or sour cream.
Preparation / Cooking Tips: If using wood skewers, soak first in water earlier than using.

GRILLED COCOA STEAK

Preparation Time: 30 minutes
Cooking Time: 10 minutes
Servings: 8

Ingredients:
1 tablespoon cocoa powder
1 1/2 tablespoons brown sugar
1 teaspoon chipotle chili powder
2 teaspoons chili powder
1/2 teaspoon onion powder
1/2 teaspoon garlic powder
1 tablespoon smoked paprika
1 tablespoon ground cumin
Salt and pepper to taste

2 lb. flank steak
Olive oil
Directions:
1. Make the dry rub with the aid of blending the cocoa powder, sugar, spices, salt and pepper.
2. Coat the flank steak with olive oil.
3. Sprinkle dry rub on both sides.
4. Preheat your Traeger wooden pellet grill too high for 15 minutes whilst the lid is closed.
5. Grill the steak for five minutes in step with side.
6. Let relaxation for 10 minutes before cutting and serving.
Serving Suggestion: Serve with mashed potatoes or green salad.
Preparation / Cooking Tips: Slice towards the grain after a few minutes of resting.

GRILLED PEPPER STEAK WITH MUSHROOM SAUCE

Preparation Time: 1 hour and 30 minutes
Cooking Time: 30 minutes
Servings: 4

Ingredients:
2 cloves garlic, minced
1 tablespoon Worcestershire sauce
1/2 cup Dijon mustard
2 tablespoons bourbon
4 tenderloin steaks
Salt and tri-color peppercorns to taste
1 tablespoon olive oil
1 onion, diced
1/2 cup white wine
1/2 cup chicken broth
16 oz. mushrooms, sliced
½ cup cream

Salt and pepper to taste
Directions:
1. In a bowl, blend the garlic, Worcestershire sauce, Dijon mustard and bourbon.
2. Spread the combination on both facets of the steak and wrap with foil.
3. Marinate in room temperature for 1 hour.
4. Unwrap and season steak with salt and peppercorns.
5. five. Press the peppercorns into the steak.
6. Preheat your Traeger wooden pellet grill to 180 ranges F for 15 minutes whilst the lid is closed.
7. Grill the steaks for 30 minutes, flipping once or twice.
8. Make the mushroom gravy by using cooking onion in olive oil in a pan over medium warmth.
9. Add mushrooms.
10. Pour within the broth and white wine.
11. Simmer for five minutes.
12. Stir within the cream.
13. Season with salt and pepper.
14. Serve steaks with sauce.
Serving Suggestion: Spread the sauce on pinnacle of the steaks and serve.
Preparation / Cooking Tips: You also can smoke the steak first for 1 hour before grilling it for an extra intense flavor.

BARBECUE PULLED PORK

Preparation Time: 1 hour and 30 minutes
Cooking Time: 8 hours
Servings: 12

Ingredients:
2 tablespoons mayonnaise

2 tablespoons mustard
1 tablespoon ketchup
1/2 teaspoon brown sugar
2 teaspoons pickle relish
10 lb. pork shoulder
6 oz. spicy dry rub
8 oz. barbecue sauce

Directions:
1. Set the Traeger timber pellet grill to smoke.
2. Preheat it for 10 minutes while the lid is closed.
3. three. Mix the mayo, mustard, ketchup, sugar, and pickles in a bowl and set aside.
4. Sprinkle all aspects of the beef shoulder with the dry rub.
5. Marinate for 45 minutes.
6. Open the lid of the wooden pellet grill and allow fire establish for 5 minutes.
7. Set it to 225 ranges F.
8. Add the pork shoulder and smoke for three hours.
9. Increase temperature to 275 stages F.
10. Roast for five hours.
11. Use a fork to shred the beef off.
12. Transfer to a bowl and stir inside the reserved sauce and fish fry sauce.

Serving Suggestion: Serve on whole wheat burger buns with tomatoes, onions and pickles.
Preparation / Cooking Tips: Use a foil pan for smoking the beef shoulder.

BARBECUE HOT DOG

Preparation Time: 10 minutes
Cooking Time: 10 minutes
Servings: 6

Ingredients:

Ingredients:
6 hot dogs
½ cup barbecue sauce
6 hot dog buns
1 onion, chopped
½ cup cheddar cheese, shredded 2

Directions:
1. Set the Traeger grill to 450 levels F.
2. Preheat whilst the lid is closed for 10 minutes.
3. Grill the hot dogs for five minutes consistent with side.
4. Brush the hot dogs with the barbeque sauce.
5. Serve inside the warm dog buns topped with the onion and cheese.

Serving Suggestion: Serve with ketchup, mustard, mayo and hot sauce.
Preparation / Cooking Tips: Use entire-wheat hot dog buns.

BARBECUE SANDWICH

Preparation Time: 30 minutes
Cooking Time: 30 minutes
Servings: 6

Ingredients:
3 lb. steak
½ cup barbecue sauce
6 ciabatta rolls
6 slices cheddar cheese

Directions:
1. Preheat your Traeger wooden pellet grill to 450 tiers F. For 15 minutes whilst the lid is closed.
2. Grill the steak for 30 minutes.
3. three. Let rest on a slicing board.
4. Slice thinly.
5. Coat with the fish fry sauce.

6. Stuff in ciabatta rolls with cheese.
Serving Suggestion: Serve with mayo or sour cream.
Preparation / Cooking Tips: You can also smoke the pork before grilling.

GRILLED LIME CHICKEN

Preparation Time: 20 minutes
Cooking Time: 45 minutes
Servings: 6

Ingredients:
2 teaspoon sugar
1 teaspoon chili powder
1 1/2 teaspoons granulated garlic
1 1/2 teaspoons ground cumin
Salt and pepper to taste
12 chicken thighs, skin removed
1 1/2 tablespoons olive oil
1 1/2 tablespoons butter
4 tablespoons pineapple juice
4 tablespoons honey
1 1/2 tablespoons lime juice
1/4 teaspoon red pepper flakes
1 1/2 tablespoons hot sauce
Directions:
1. Set the Traeger grill to 375 degrees F.
2. Preheat it for 10 minutes.
3. three. In a bowl, mix the sugar, chili powder, garlic, cumin, salt and pepper.
4. Coat the bird with the olive oil and sprinkle with the dry rub.
5. Grill the chicken for 7 minutes according to side.
6. In a pan over medium warmness, simmer the rest of the elements for 10 minutes.
7. Remove from warmness and transfer to a bowl.
8. Brush the mixture on each sides of the

hen.
9. Cook for any other 7 minutes in step with side.
Serving Suggestion: Garnish with lime wedges.
Preparation / Cooking Tips: Add more hot sauce to the glaze if you want your chicken spicier.

BARBECUE PORK BELLY

Preparation Time: 15 minutes
Cooking Time: 3 hours
Servings: 6

Ingredients:
3 lb. pork belly
Salt and pepper to taste Barbecue dry rub
Directions:
1. Preheat your Traeger wood pellet grill to 275 levels F for 15 minutes while the lid is closed.
2. Sprinkle all sides of pork stomach with salt, pepper and dry rub.
3. Cook for three hours.
4. Let rest for 10 minutes before cutting and serving.
Serving Suggestion: Serve with rice, salad or bread.
Preparation / Cooking Tips: You can also coat with barbecue sauce before serving.

SMOKING RECIPES

SMOKED RIBS

Preparation Time: 20 minutes
Cooking Time: 6 hours
Servings: 8

Ingredients:
4 baby back ribs
1 cup pork rub
1 cup barbecue sauce
Directions:
1.Preheat your grill to 180 tiers F for 15 mins at the same time as the lid is closed.
2. Sprinkle toddler again ribs with beef rub.
3. Smoke the ribs for 5 hours.
4. Brush the ribs with barbecue sauce.
5. Wrap the ribs with foil.
6. Put the ribs again to the grill.
7. increase temperature to 350 levels F.
8. Cook for forty-five mins to at least one hour.
9. Let rest before slicing and serving.
Serving Suggestion: Serve with steamed veggies.
Preparation / Cooking Tips: Trim excess fats from the toddler lower back ribs earlier than cooking

CAJUN SHRIMP

Preparation Time: 3 hours and 15 minutes
Cooking Time: 10 minutes
Servings: 4

Ingredients:
4 tablespoons olive oil
1 tablespoon lemon juice
2 cloves garlic, minced
1 tablespoon Cajun rub
Salt to taste
2 lb. shrimp, peeled and deveined
Directions:
1. Mix all of the ingredients in a bowl.
2. Cover the bowl and refrigerate for three hours.
3. Set the Traeger grill to excessive and preheat for 15 minutes while the lid is closed.
4. four. Thread the shrimp onto skewers.
5. Grill the shrimp for four mins consistent with side.
Serving Suggestion: Serve with sour cream or herbed mayo dipping sauce.
Preparation / Cooking Tips: If using wood skewers, soak first in water for 15 mins earlier than using.

SMOKED CHEESE DIP

Preparation Time: 40 minutes
Cooking Time: 1 hour and 15 minutes
Servings: 8

Ingredients:
Ice cubes
1 block cheddar cheese 8 tablespoons butter
½ cup carrots, chopped
1 onion, chopped
1 cup heavy cream
3/4 cup flour
Hot sauce
1 teaspoon Worcestershire sauce
Directions:

1. Preheat your Traeger timber pellet grill to 180 stages F for 15 mins while the lid is closed.
2. Add ice cubes to a pan.
3. Place a cooling rack on pinnacle.
4. Put the cheese block on the rack.
5. Put this on pinnacle of the grill.
6. Smoke for 30 mins.
7. Transfer the cheese in your freezer.
8. In a pan over medium heat, upload the butter and let it melt.
9. Cook the onion and carrots for 15 minutes.
10. Stir within the rest of the components.
11. Reduce warmth and simmer for 15 mins.
12. Take the cheese out of the freezer and shred.
13. Put the shredded cheese into the combination.
14. Stir whilst cooking till cheese has melted.

Serving Suggestion: Serve with chips, crackers or vegetable dippers.

Preparation / Cooking Tips: You also can upload herbs to the cheese dip if you like.

SMOKED POT ROAST

Preparation Time: 30 minutes
Cooking Time: 6 hours
Servings: 4

Ingredients:
Salt and pepper to taste
1 teaspoon onion powder
1 teaspoon garlicpowder
3 lb. chuck roast

2 cups potatoes, sliced in half
2 cups carrots, sliced
2 onions, peeled
1 teaspoon chili powder
1 cup red wine
1 tablespoon fresh rosemary, chopped
1 tablespoon fresh thyme, chopped
2 dried chipotle peppers
2 cups beef stock

Directions:
1. Mix salt, pepper, onion powder and garlic powder in a bowl.
2. Rub chuck roast with this aggregate.
3. three. Preheat your Traeger timber pellet grill to 180 ranges F for 15 mins while the lid is closed.
4. Smoke the pork for 1 hour.
5. Increase temperature to 275 tiers F.
6. Place the pork and the relaxation of the ingredients in a Dutch oven.
7. Seal the Dutch oven and area on the grill.
8. Braise for five hours.

Serving Suggestion: Serve with roasted vegetables and gravy.

Preparation / Cooking Tips: You can also use dried herbs in place of clean herbs.

SMOKED TURKEY

Preparation Time: 1 day and 1 hour
Cooking Time: 4 hours and 30 minutes
Servings: 6

Ingredients:
2 gallons' water, divided
2 cups sugar
2 cups salt
Ice cubes
1 whole turkey

½ cup kosher salt
½ cup black pepper
3 sticks butter, sliced

Directions:
1. Add one-quart water to a pot over medium warmth.
2. Stir in the 2 cups each of sugar and salt.
3. Bring to a boil.
4. Remove from warmth and allow cool.
5. Add ice and the last water.
6. Stir to cool.
7. Add the turkey to the brine.
8. Cover and refrigerate for 24 hours.
9. Rinse the turkey and dry with paper towels.
10.   Season with salt and pepper.
11.   Preheat the Traeger timber pellet grill to 180 stages F for 15 mins at the same time as the lid is closed.
12.   Smoke the turkey for 2 hours.
13.   Increase temperature to 225 stages. Smoke for every other 1 hour.
14.   Increase temperature to 325 tiers. Smoke for 30 mins.
15.   Place the turkey on pinnacle of a foil sheet.
16.   Add butter on top of the turkey.
17.   Cover the turkey with foil.
18.   Reduce temperature to 165 degrees F.
19.   Cook on the grill for 1 hour.

Serving Suggestion: Serve with mashed potatoes and gravy.

Preparation / Cooking Tips: Prepare and trim the turkey before getting ready the brine.

SMOKED BRISKET

Preparation Time: 30 minutes
Cooking Time: 12 hours

Servings: 8

Ingredients:
Salt and pepper to taste
2 tablespoons beef rub
1 tablespoon Worcestershire sauce
6 lb. brisket
1 cup beef broth

Directions:
11. Mix salt, pepper, beef rub and Worcestershire sauce in a bowl.
2. Rub brisket with this combination.
3. Preheat your Traeger timber pellet grill to 180 levels F for 15 minutes while the lid is closed.
4. Smoke the brisket for 7 hours.
5. Transfer brisket on top of a foil.
6. Pour the broth over the brisket.
7. Wrap it with foil.
8. Smoke for five hours.
9. Let rest before slicing.

Serving Suggestion: Serve with barbecue sauce.

Preparation / Cooking Tips: Slice against the grain.

SMOKED POTATOES

Preparation Time: 30 minutes
Cooking Time: 1 hour
Servings: 6

Ingredients:
2 tablespoon butter
1/2 cup milk
1 cup heavy cream
2 cloves garlic, crushed and minced
2 tablespoons flour
4 potatoes, sliced thinly
Salt and pepper to taste

1 cup cheddar cheese, grated
Directions:
1. Preheat your Traeger timber pellet grill to 375 levels F for 15 minutes at the same time as the lid is closed.
2. Add butter for your forged iron pan.
3. In a bowl, blend the milk, cream, garlic and flour.
4. Arrange some of the potatoes in a pan.
5. Season with salt and pepper.
6. Pour some of the sauce over the potatoes.
7. Repeat layers till elements were used.
8. Grill for 50 minutes.
Sprinkle cheese on top and prepare dinner for 10 minutes.
Serving Suggestion: Garnish with chopped parsley before serving.
Preparation / Cooking Tips: Soak the potatoes in water to keep away from discoloration.

SMOKED TUNA

Preparation Time: 6 hours and 15 minutes
Cooking Time: 3 hours
Servings: 6

Ingredients:
2 cups water
1 cup brown sugar
1 cup salt
1 tablespoon lemon zest
6 tuna fillets
Directions:
1. Mix water, brown sugar, salt and lemon zest in a bowl.
2. Coat the tuna fillets with the combination.
3. Refrigerate for six hours.

4. Rinse the tuna and pat dry with paper towels.
5. Preheat the Traeger wood pellet grill to 180 degrees F for 15 mins even as the lid is closed.
6. Smoke the tuna for three hours.
Serving Suggestion: Serve with buttered corn.
Preparation / Cooking Tips: You can also soak tuna in the brine for 24 hours.

SMOKED MUSHROOMS

Preparation Time: 30 minutes
Cooking Time: 45 minutes
Servings: 4

Ingredients:
4 cups Portobello mushrooms
1 tablespoon oil
1 teaspoon onion powder
1 teaspoon granulated garlic Salt and pepper to taste
Directions:
1. Add all the substances in a huge bowl.
2. Mix well.
3. Preheat your Traeger wooden pellet grill to 180 ranges F.
4. Smoke the mushrooms for 30 mins.
5. Increase temperature to 200 stages F and smoke for every other 15 minutes.
Serving Suggestion: Sprinkle with chopped herbs earlier than serving.
Preparation / Cooking Tips: You can also use other types of mushrooms for this recipe.

SMOKED DEVILED EGGS

Preparation Time: 30 minutes

Cooking Time: 45 minutes
Servings: 12

Ingredients:
12 hard-boiled eggs, peeled and sliced in half
2 jalapeño peppers
2 slices bacon, cooked crisp and chopped
1/2 cup mayonnaise
2 teaspoons white vinegar
2 teaspoon mustard
1/2 teaspoon chili powder
1/2 teaspoon paprika
Salt to taste
Pinch paprika
Chopped chives

Directions:
1. With the roasted peppers.
2. Serving Set the Traeger wood pellet grill to 180 ranges F.
3. Preheat for 15 minutes while the lid is closed.
4. Smoke the eggs and peppers for forty-five minutes.
5. Transfer to a plate.
6. Scoop out the egg yolks and location in a bowl.
7. Stir in the rest of the substances.
8. Mash the eggs and blend well.
9. Scoop the egg combination on top of the egg whites.
Serve Suggestion: Serve as appetizer.
Preparation / Cooking Tips: Add vinegar in your water when boiling the eggs to make them less difficult to peel.

ROASTING/BAKING RECIPES

ROASTED LAMB

Preparation Time: 10 hours and 30 minutes
Cooking Time: 1 hour and 30 minutes
Servings: 8

Ingredients:
1 leg of lamb
8 cloves garlic, minced
1 sprig oregano, chopped
2 sprigs rosemary, chopped
6 tablespoons olive oil
2 tablespoons lemon juice
Salt and pepper to taste

Directions:
1. Make slits at the lamb leg.
2. Combine the garlic and herbs.
3. Mash to shape a paste.
4. Stuff aggregate within the slits.
5. Add the lamb leg to a roasting pan.
6. Drizzle it with olive oil and lemon juice.
7. Cover with foil and refrigerate for 10 hours.
8. When ready to cook, sprinkle lamb with salt and pepper.
9. Set the Traeger wood pellet grill to 400 ranges F.
10. Preheat for 15 minutes while the lid is closed.
11. Open the lid and permit it establish fire for five minutes.
12. Roast the leg of lamb for 30 mins.

13. Reduce temperature to 350 stages F and prepare dinner for 1 hour.

14. Let relaxation earlier than slicing and serving.

Serving Suggestion: Garnish with lemon wedges.

Preparation / Cooking Tips: You can also use a meals processor to create a paste from the garlic and herbs.

ROASTED PORK WITH STRAWBERRY

Preparation Time: 40 minutes
Cooking Time: 1 hour
Servings: 4

Ingredients:
2 lb. pork tenderloin
2 tablespoons dried rosemary
Salt and pepper to taste
2 tablespoons olive oil
12 strawberries
1 cup balsamic vinegar
4 tablespoons sugar

Directions:
1. Preheat your Traeger wood pellet grill to 350 stages F for 15 minutes even as the lid is closed.

2. Season the beef tenderloin with rosemary, salt and pepper.

3. In a pan over excessive warmth, sear the tenderloin for two mins in line with side.

4. Place the pan in the grill and prepare dinner for 20 mins.

5. Transfer to a reducing board.

6. In some other pan, simmer the strawberries in sugar and vinegar for 30 minutes.

7. Slice the beef and pour with the sauce

earlier than se

8. rving.

Serving Suggestion: Garnish with herb sprigs.

Preparation / Cooking Tips: You can also chop the strawberries before cooking.

ROASTED ALMONDS

Preparation Time: 20 minutes
Cooking Time: 1 hour and 30 minutes
Servings: 6

Ingredients:
1 egg white Salt to taste
1 tablespoon ground cinnamon
1 cup granulated sugar
1 lb. almonds

Directions:
1. Beat the egg white in a bowl till frothy.

2. Stir in salt, cinnamon and sugar.

3. Coat the almonds with this mixture.

4. four. Spread almonds on a baking pan.

5. five. Set your Traeger wood pellet grill to 225 degrees F.

6. Preheat for 15 mins at the same time as the lid is closed.

7. Roast the almonds for 90 minutes, stirring each 1

8. 0 mins.

Other Tips: Store in an airtight field with lid for up to at least one week.

ROASTED HAM

Preparation Time: 1 day and 40 minutes
Cooking Time: 6 hours
Servings: 12

Ingredients:

2 quarts' water
1/2 cup quick home meat cure
1/2 cup kosher salt
3/4 cup brown sugar
1 tablespoon pork rub
1 teaspoon whole cloves
10 lb. fresh ham
1 teaspoon whole cloves
1/4 cup pure maple syrup
2 cup apple juice

Directions:
1. In a massive box, pour within the water and add the beef cure, salt, sugar, beef rub and complete cloves.
2. Mix well.
3. Soak the ham inside the brine.
4. Cover and refrigerate for 1 day.
5. five. Rinse ham with water and dry with paper towels.
6. Score the ham with crosshatch pattern.
7. Insert final cloves into the ham.
8. Season ham with the red meat rub.
9. Add ham to a roasting pan.
10. Smoke the ham in the Traeger wood pellet grill for 2 hours at 180 degrees F.
11. Make the glaze by mixing the maple syrup and apple juice.
12. Brush the ham with this mixture.
13. Increase heat to 300 stages F.
14. Roast for 4 hours.

Serving Suggestion: Serve with crusty bread.
Preparation / Cooking Tips: You can also inject the brine into the ham.

ROASTED WINGS

Preparation Time: 30 minutes
Cooking Time: 1 hour
Servings: 6

Ingredients:
4 lb. chicken wings
1 tablespoon cornstarch
Salt to taste
Chicken rub
6 tablespoon butter
1/2 cup hot sauce
1/4 cup spicy mustard

Directions:
1. Preheat the Traeger wood pellet grill to 375 levels F for 15 mins at the same time as the lid is closed.
2. In a bowl, blend the cornstarch, salt and fowl rub.
3. Sprinkle the chook with this aggregate.
4. Roast the bird for 16 minutes per side.
5. five. In a pot over medium heat, simmer the relaxation of the substances for 15 mins.
6. Dip the wings within the butter aggregate.
7. Cook for 10 greater mins.

Serving Suggestion: Serve with blue cheese dressing.
Preparation / Cooking Tips: Pat the chicken wings dry with paper towels earlier than seasoning.

CRISPY FISH STICKS

Preparation Time: 20 minutes
Cooking Time: 5 minutes
Servings: 6

Ingredients:
Olive oil
1 ½ lb. halibut, sliced into strips
1/2 cup all-purpose flour
Salt and pepper to taste
2 eggs, beaten

1 1/2 cup panko breadcrumbs
2 tablespoon dried parsley
1 teaspoon dried dill weed
1/2 cup hot sauce
1/4 cup spicy mustard

Directions:
1. Preheat the Traeger timber pellet grill to excessive for 15 minutes even as the lid is closed.
2. Pour olive oil to a pan.
3. Add pan on top of the grill.
4. Add flour, salt and pepper to a bowl. Mix well.
5. five. Add the eggs to any other bowl.
6. In every other bowl, mix the breadcrumbs and herbs.
7. Dip the fish strips inside the flour combination, eggs and breadcrumb combination.
8. Place in oil and fry for 5 mins or till golden.

Serving Suggestion: Sprinkle with chopped
parsley before serving.

Preparation / Cooking Tips: Beat the egg white first till frothy earlier than stirring in egg yolk. This makes it easier for breadcrumbs to paste to the fish.

DINNER ROLLS

Preparation Time: 40 minutes
Cooking Time: 10 minutes Servings: 12

Ingredients:
2 tablespoons active dry yeast
1/3 cup vegetable oil
1 1/10 cup warm water (115 degrees F)
1/4 cup sugar
1 egg, beaten

Pinch salt
3 1/2 cups all-purpose flour Cooking spray

Directions:
1. Set the Traeger wooden pellet grill to 400 ranges F.
2. Preheat for 15 minutes while the lid is closed.
3. Use a stand mixer to combine dry yeast, oil, heat water and sugar.
4. four. Let it rest for 10 minutes.
5. Stir inside the egg, salt and flour.
6. Spray cast iron pan with oil.
7. Knead the dough and form into 12 balls.
8. Place the balls on the pan.
9. Let relaxation for 10 minutes.
10. Bake inside the wooden pellet grill for 10 mins.

Serving Suggestion: Serve with your choice of stuffing: cheese, ham or burger patty.

Preparation / Cooking Tips: You also can mix manually in case you don't have a mixer.

BAKED BREAKFAST CASSEROLE

Preparation Time: 40 minutes
Cooking Time: 1 hour
Servings: 8

Ingredients:
6 bread slices, cut into cubes
6 eggs
3/4 teaspoon ground mustard
1 cup milk
Salt and pepper to taste
1 onion, chopped
1 bell pepper, chopped

6 ounces' chorizo
6 ounces ground turkey
1 cup baby spinach
4 slices bacon, cooked crispy and chopped into bits
1 cup Swiss cheese, grated
2 cups cheddar cheese, grated

Directions:

1. Set the Traeger timber pellet grill to 350 degrees F.
2. Preheat for 15 mins at the same time as the lid is closed.
3. Spray your baking pan with oil.
4. Arrange the bread cubes inside the baking pan.
5. Beat the eggs in a bowl.
6. Stir in the mustard, milk, salt and pepper.
7. Spray your pan with oil.
8. Place the pan over medium warmth.
9. Cook the onion, bell pepper, ground turkey and chorizo.
10. Stir inside the spinach.
11. Cook for 1 minute.
12. Place the meat aggregate on top of the bread.
13. Pour egg combination on top.
14. Sprinkle cheeses on pinnacle.
15. Repeat layers.
16. Cover the baking pan with foil.
17. Bake inside the wooden pellet grill for 40 mins.
18. Remove cowl and bake for another 10 mins.

Serving Suggestion: Sprinkle with chopped
parsley earlier than serving.

Preparation / Cooking Tips: You can also cook dinner floor turkey and chorizo in advance to much less training time.

BAKED ASPARAGUS & BACON

Preparation Time: 40 minutes
Cooking Time: 1 hour
Servings: 8

Ingredients:

3 eggs
1 cup heavy cream
1 tablespoon chopped fresh chives
1/4 cup goat cheese
4 tablespoons Parmesan cheese
8 oz. fresh asparagus, trimmed
8 oz. bacon, cooked crispy and chopped
¼ teaspoon lemon zest

Directions:

1. Preheat the Traeger wooden pellet grill to 375 degrees F for 15 mins while the lid is closed.
2. In a bowl, beat the eggs and stir in cream, chives, goat cheese and Parmesan cheese.
3. Arrange the asparagus in a baking pan.
4. Spread cream aggregate on pinnacle.
5. Sprinkle bacon bits and lemon zest on pinnacle.
6. Bake for 20 minutes.

Serving Suggestion: Garnish with shaved Parmesan cheese.

Preparation / Cooking Tips: You can also use this recipe for other greens like broccoli.

BAKED APPLE CRISP

Preparation Time: 40 minutes
Cooking Time: 30 minutes
Servings: 7

Ingredients:
Butter for greasing
1/2 cup flour
1/2 cup rolled oats
1 stick butter, sliced into cubes
1 cup brown sugar
1 1/2 teaspoon ground cinnamon
1/4 cup walnuts, chopped
3 lb. apples, sliced thinly
½ cup dried cranberries
2 1/2 tablespoons bourbon
1/2 cup brown sugar
1 tablespoon lemon juice
1/4 cup honey
1 teaspoon vanilla
1 1/2 teaspoons ground cinnamon
Pinch salt

Directions:
1. Grease forged iron pan with butter.
2. Add flour, oats, butter cubes, 1 cup sugar, cinnamon and walnuts to a meals processor. Pulse until crumbly.
3. In a bowl, blend the apples with the rest of the ingredients.
4. Pour apple mixture into the greased pan.
5. Spread flour combination on top.
6. Bake within the Traeger timber pellet grill at 350 degrees F for 1 hour.

Serving Suggestion: Serve with vanilla ice cream.

Preparation / Cooking Tips: Use freshly squeezed lemon juice.

MEAT RECIPES

PORTERHOUSE STEAK

Preparation Time: 30 minutes
Cooking Time: 35 minutes
Servings: 4

Ingredients:
2 tablespoon Worcestershire sauce
2 teaspoon Dijon mustard
4 tablespoon butter
Prime rib rub
2 porterhouse steaks

Directions:
1. Preheat your Traeger timber pellet grill to 225 stages F for 15 minutes whilst the lid is closed.
2. In a bowl, mix the Worcestershire sauce, mustard and butter.
3. Brush steaks with this combination.
4. Sprinkle with the dry rub.
5. Grill for 30 minutes, flipping once.
6. Increase temperature for 500 ranges F and grill for 2 mins consistent with side.

Serving Suggestion: Serve with mashed potatoes and gravy.

Preparation / Cooking Tips: Choose steaks that are at the least 1 ½ inch thick.

STRIP STEAK WITH ONION SAUCE

Preparation Time: 40 minutes
Cooking Time: 1 hour
Servings: 4

Ingredients:

2 New York strip steaks
Prime rib rub
½ lb. bacon, chopped
1 onion, sliced
1/4 cup brown sugar
1/2 tablespoon balsamic vinegar
3 tablespoons brewed coffee
1/4 cup apple juice

Directions:
1. Sprinkle each aspects of steaks with high rib rub.
2. Set the Traeger wood pellet grill to 350 levels F.
3. Preheat for 15 minutes at the same time as the lid is closed.
4. Place a pan over the grill.
5. Cook the bacon until crispy.
6. Transfer to a plate.
7. Cook the onion in the bacon drippings for 10 mins.
8. Stir in brown sugar and cook for 20 mins.
9. Add the relaxation of the substances and prepare dinner for 20 mins.
10. Grill the steaks for 5 mins in line with side.
11. Serve with the onion and bacon combination.

Serving Suggestion: Serve with buttered vegetables.

Preparation / Cooking Tips: Ensure steak is in room temperature before seasoning.

COWBOY STEAK

Preparation Time: 30 minutes
Cooking Time: 1 hour
Servings: 4

Ingredients:

lb. cowboy cut steaks
Salt to taste
Beef rub
1/4 cup olive oil
2 tablespoons fresh mint leaves, chopped
½ cup parsley, chopped
1 clove garlic, crushed and minced
1 tablespoon lemon juice
1 tablespoon lemon zest
Salt and pepper to taste

Directions:
1. Season the steak with the salt and dry rub.
2. Preheat the Traeger timber pellet grill to 225 ranges F for 10 mins at the same time as the lid is closed.
3. Grill the steaks for forty-five mins, flipping as soon as or twice.
4. Increase temperature to 450 stages F.
5. Put the steaks again to the grill. Cook for 5 mins according to side.
6. In a bowl, mix the ultimate ingredients.
7. Serve steaks with the parsley combination.

Serving Suggestion: Serve with fresh inexperienced salad.

Preparation / Cooking Tips: Let steak relaxation for 10 minutes earlier than putting it back to the grill for the second one round of cooking.

SUNDAY-BEST PORK LOIN ROAST WITH THYME-FIG BALSAMIC MARINADE

Servings: 4 to 8

Ingredients:
3 ½ cup fig balsamic vinegar
½ cup olive oil

6 cloves garlic, finely chopped
3 tablespoons chopped fresh thyme
1 tablespoon Dijon mustard
1 teaspoon kosher salt
1 teaspoon fennel seeds
Freshly ground black pepper
1 (3- to 4-pound) center-cut boneless p
ork loin roast
6 cloves garlic, finely chopped
3 tablespoons chopped fresh thyme
1 tablespoon Dijon mustard
1 teaspoon kosher salt
1 teaspoon fennel seeds
Freshly ground black pepper
1 (3- to 4-pound) center-cut boneless p
ork loin roast

Directions:

1. In a small bowl, whisk the vinegar, oil, garlic, thyme, mustard, salt, fennel seeds, and 5 grindings of black pepper collectively. Place the pork roast in a 2^-gallon zip-pinnacle plastic bag. Add the marinade, seal the bag, and squish the marinade round the red meat to coat. Refrigerate for at the least 24 hours; 48 is better. Turn the bag frequently.

2. Remove the beef from the marinade at least 45 minutes before cooking; reserve the marinade. Let the pork stand at room temperature.

3. Light a hearth in the kamado grill the usage of your favored method. After approximately 10 minutes, area the grill rack in position, close the dome, and open the upper and decrease dampers all of the manner. When the temperature reaches 400° F, adjust the dampers to keep the temperature.

4. Insert the ceramic plate in the kamado and area the roast at the grill, or set the pork roast on a rack in a roasting pan, and place the pan on the grill. Close the dome and adjust the dampers for a grill temperature of 375° F. Roast for about 20 minutes, then brush the red meat with the reserved marinade. Cook for every other 45 to 60 mins for a medium doneness; the internal temperature has to be between 145° and 150° F.

5. Transfer the pork to a slicing board and let relaxation for 15 mins. Cut into ^-inch-thick slices and serve heat or at room temperature.

CROWN ROAST OF PORK WITH APPLE-CHESTNUT SAUSAGE STUFFING

Servings: 6 to 8

Lease resist the urge to put little "chop hats" on the bones of this roast, unless you're serving it up at a retro-themed dinner party. You will probably need to order the roast in advance. If a crown roast is a little over the top for you, or you don't have many folks to feed, order a bone-in pork loin (a crown roast is two bone-in pork loins tied together) and cook the stuffing alongside the roast.

This is an easy recipe to make you own. You can use whatever type of sausage you prefer, swap pecans and/or walnuts for the pistachios, and feel free to leave out the chestnuts entirely if you can't find them or don't like them.

Ingredients:

Grated zest and juice of 2 oranges
Grated zest and juice of 1 lemon
1 tablespoon kosher salt

1 (8- to 10-pound) crown roast of pork
1 tablespoon unsalted butter
1 tablespoon olive oil
1 ½ cup chopped onion
2 ribs celery, chopped
1 tart apple, peeled, cored, and finely chopped
1-pound bulk country pork sausage
8 ounces jarred or canned peeled chestnuts, drained and coarsely chopped
½ cup shelled unsalted pistachio nuts
8 cups cubed day-old French bread
3 to 4 cups low-sodium chicken broth or equal parts apple cider and broth
½ cup finely chopped shallots
4 cloves garlic, run through a press
1½ teaspoon ground fennel seeds
1 to 2 tablespoons all-purpose flour or gravy flour

Directions:

1. In a small bowl, integrate the zests and salt. Rub the combination all around the roast, inner and out. Set the roast in a huge cast-iron skillet.
2. In a huge sauté pan over medium warmth, warmness the butter and oil. When the butter foams, add the onion, celery, and apple and cook dinner until softened, approximately five minutes, stirring a few times. Crumble the sausage into the pan and prepare dinner until it's miles browned and no red remains. Pour the sausage mixture into a large bowl. Add the nuts, bread, and citrus juices and toss to integrate. Add 1 to 2 cups of the broth to moisten; the aggregate should live together whilst pinched. Let the stuffing cool off until no steam is growing from the bowl. Firmly % the stuffing into the middle of

the crown roast.
3. Light a hearth within the kamado grill the use of your favorite method. After about 10 minutes, vicinity the grill rack in position, near the dome, and open the upper and decrease dampers all the manner. When the temperature reaches 450° F, alter the dampers to keep the temperature.
4. Place the skillet at the grill and near the dome. Roast for about 30 minutes.
5. Adjust the dampers to drop the grill temperature to approximately 325° F. Continue to roast the red meat till internal temperature of the beef (no longer the stuffing) is 140° to 145° F.
6. Transfer the roast to a cutting board, loosely tent with aluminum foil, and allow it rest for 25 to 30 minutes. Meanwhile, vicinity the skillet over medium warmness at the stovetop, upload the shallots, garlic, fennel, and flour, and cook, stirring, till the shallots are barely colored, five to 10 mins. Pour in 2 cups broth and scrape the lowest of the pan to get up all the browned bits. Bring to a boil, then reduce the heat to a simmer and permit bubble till the sauce has the desired thickness. Strain the sauce through a first-rate mesh strainer and keep heat. Carve the roast among the ribs and serve with the stuffing and pan gravy.

ROASTED PORK LOIN STUFFED WITH BACON- ONION JAM, MASCARPONE, APRICOTS, AND PLUMS

Servings: 6 to 8

You need to start this recipe a day or

two before you plan to serve it if you are going to make the bacon jam, which I highly recommend you do. This is a perfect dish for a holiday centerpiece or for whenever you have a taste for something out of the ordinary.

Ingredients:
1 (4- to 5-pound) boneless center-cut pork loin roast
1½ cup Bacon-Onion Jam or store-bought onion jam
1½ cup mascarpone cheese
12 to 14 dried apricots
12 to 14 dried plums (prunes)
Kosher salt and freshly ground black pepper
Kitchen twine
Apricot jam, slightly melted so it's easy to brush

Directions:
1. Slice the red meat roast lengthwise but no longer all the manner thru. Open the roast up and then slice both aspects in 1/2 in order that the red meat roast lies open like a book. Take care no longer to reduce any of the beef all of the manner through.
2. Smear the insides of the red meat roast with the bacon-onion jam. Spread the mascarpone over the jam after which top with the apricots and dried plums, spreading them evenly for the duration of the roast. Season with salt and pepper. Roll the roast tightly collectively lengthwise and tie at 1-inch durations with kitchen twine. Let take a seat at room temperature even as you begin your fireplace.
3. Light a fire within the kamado grill using your favorite method. After about 10 minutes, region the grill rack in position, near the dome, and open the top and

lower dampers all the manner. When the temperature reaches 400° F, regulate the dampers to preserve the temperature.
4. Insert the ceramic plate in the kamado or set the roast on a rack in a roasting pan and place the pan at the grill. Close the dome and regulate the temperature downward to 375° F. Roast for approximately 1 hour, then brush with the apricot jam. Continue to prepare dinner approximately another 20 mins, brushing once more with the jam towards the give up of that time. The roast is prepared when the internal temperature is among 140° and 150° F.
5. Transfer the red meat to a slicing board and permit rest for 15 minutes. Cut into ^-inch-thick slices and serve warm or at room temperature.

SMOKED PRIME RIB

Preparation Time: 1 hour
Cooking Time: 5 hours
Servings: 12

Ingredients:
10 lb. rib eye roast
Salt to taste
Barbecue rub
Garlic and herb seasoning
Worcestershire sauce
Beef stock
3 tablespoons butter

Directions:
1. Preheat the Traeger wooden pellet grill to 275 degrees F for 15 minutes even as the lid is closed.
2. Sprinkle the roast with salt, rub, and garlic and herb seasoning.

3. Marinate for 20 minutes.
4. Add the rib roast to the grill.
5. Smoke for five hours, basting with a mixture of Worcestershire sauce and red meat inventory every 45 minutes.
6. Transfer to a plate.
7. Add the butter to the roast and allow it melt.
8. Serve after five minutes.
Serving Suggestion: Serve with mashed potatoes and gravy.
Preparation / Cooking Tips: Use boneless rib-eye roast for this recipe.

ROAST BEEF

Preparation Time: 30 minutes
Cooking Time: 5 hours Servings: 8

Ingredients:
5 lb. sirloin roast
1 tablespoon olive oil
Prime rib dry rub
Directions:
1. Tie the sirloin roast with kitchen string.
2. Brush the roast with oil and season with dry rub.
3. Set the Traeger wooden pellet grill to 180 levels F.
4. Roast the beef for five hours.
5. Remove the kitchen string.
6. Let cool before slicing thinly.
Serving Suggestion: Serve with rice or salad, or as sandwich.
Preparation / Cooking Tips: Use a meat slicer to slice the red meat extra easily

SWEET & SPICY PORK ROAST

Preparation Time: 1 day and 40 minutes
Cooking Time: 1 hour and 30 minutes
Servings: 4

Ingredients:
3 lb. pork loin
1/2 teaspoon Chinese 5 spice
1 can coconut milk
1 habanero pepper
1 teaspoon curry powder
1 tablespoon paprika
1 teaspoon ginger, grated
1 tablespoon garlic, minced
1 tablespoon lime juice
Directions:
1. Place red meat in a bowl.
2. In some other bowl, combine the closing elements.
3. three. Pour the combination over the beef and marinate in a single day covered within the refrigerator.
4. Set the Traeger wooden pellet grill to 300 levels F.
5. Preheat for 15 mins while the lid is closed.
6. Add the beef to the grill.
7. Cook for 1 hour.
8. Flip and cook dinner for any other 30 minutes.
Serving Suggestion: Serve with hot brown rice.
Preparation / Cooking Tips: You also can marinate for at least 4 hours.

ROASTED PORK WITH BLACKBERRY SAUCE

Preparation Time: 30 minutes
Cooking Time: 50 minutes Servings: 4

Ingredients:
2 lb. pork tenderloin
2 tablespoons dried rosemary
Salt and pepper to taste
2 tablespoons olive oil
12 blackberries, sliced
1 cup balsamic vinegar
4 tablespoons sugar

Directions:
1. Preheat the Traeger timber pellet grill to 350 degrees F for 15 mins even as the lid is closed.
2. Season the red meat with the rosemary, salt and pepper.
3. In a pan over high heat, pour in the oil and sear beef for 2 mins according to side.
4. Transfer to the grill and prepare dinner for 20 minutes.
5. Take the pan off the grill.
6. Let relaxation for 10 minutes.
7. In a pan over medium warmness, simmer the blackberries in vinegar and sugar for 30 mins.
8. Pour sauce over the beef and serve.

Serving Suggestion: Serve with inexperienced salad.

Preparation / Cooking Tips: You also can simmer the beef inside the blackberry sauce for 10 mins.

CITRUS PORK CHOPS

Preparation Time: 3 hours and 30 minutes
Cooking Time: 30 minutes Servings: 4

Ingredients:
2 oranges, sliced into wedges
2 lemons, sliced into wedges
6 sprigs rosemary, chopped
2 sticks butter, softened
1 clove garlic, minced
4 tablespoons fresh thyme leaves, chopped
1 teaspoon black pepper
5 pork chops

Directions:
1. Set the Traeger timber pellet grill to smoke.
2. Wait for it to set up fireplace for five minutes.
3. Set temperature to high.
4. Squeeze lemons and oranges into a bowl.
5. Stir within the relaxation of the elements besides the beef chops.
6. Marinate the pork chops within the aggregate for three hours.
7. Grill for 10 minutes in line with side. Serve with brown rice or mushroom gravy. Use bone-in beef chops for this recipe.

LAMB LEG WITH SALSA

Preparation Time: 40 minutes
Cooking Time: 1 hour and 30 minutes
Servings: 6

Ingredients:
6 cloves garlic, peeled and sliced
1 leg of lamb
Salt and pepper to taste

2 tablespoons fresh rosemary, chopped
Olive oil
3 cups salsa

Directions:

1. Set the Traeger timber pellet grill to excessive.
2. Preheat for 15 mins while the lid is closed.
3. Make slits all over the lamb leg.
4. Insert the garlic slices.
5. Drizzle with oil and rub with salt, pepper and rosemary.
6. Marinate for 30 minutes.
7. Set temperature to 350 stages F.
8. Cook lamb leg for 1 hour and 30 minutes.
9. Serve with salsa.
10. Garnish with lemon wedges.
11. You can also insert whole garlic cloves into the slits.

BRAISED LAMB

Preparation Time: 50 minutes
Cooking Time: 3 hours and 20 minutes
Servings: 4

Ingredients:
4 lamb shanks
Prime rib rub
1 cup red wine
1 cup beef broth
2 sprigs thyme
2 sprigs rosemary

Directions:

1. Sprinkle all facets of lamb shanks with top rib rub.
2. Set temperature of the timber pellet grill to high.
3. Preheat it for 15 mins at the same time as the lid is closed.
4. Add the lamb to the grill and cook dinner for 20 mins.
5. five. Transfer the lamb to a Dutch oven.
6. Stir inside the rest of the components.
7. Transfer again to the grill.
8. Reduce temperature to 325 stages F.
9. Braise the lamb for three hours.
Serve with garlic potatoes.
Let cool before serving

POULTRY RECIPES

LEMON CHICKEN

Preparation Time: 4 hours and 30 minutes
Cooking Time: 10 minutes
Servings: 6

Ingredients:
2 teaspoons honey
1 tablespoon lemon juice
1 teaspoon lemon zest
1 clove garlic, coarsely chopped
2 sprigs thyme
Salt and pepper to taste
½ cup olive oil
6 chicken breast fillets

Directions:

1. Mix the honey, lemon juice, lemon zest, garlic, thyme, salt and pepper in a bowl.
2. Gradually add olive oil to the combination.
3. Soak the chook fillets in the combination.
4. Cover and refrigerate for 4 hours.
5. Preheat the Traeger timber pellet grill to

400 degrees F for 15 mins even as the lid is closed.

6. Grill the chook for 5 minutes in step with side.

Serving Suggestion: Garnish with lemon wedges.

Preparation / Cooking Tips: You can also make additional marinade for use for basting all through grill time.

HONEY GARLIC CHICKEN WINGS

Preparation Time: 30 minutes
Cooking Time: 1 hour and 15 minutes
Servings: 4

Ingredients:
2 1/2 lb. chicken wings
Poultry dry rub
4 tablespoons butter
3 cloves garlic, minced
1/2 cup hot sauce
1/4 cup honey
Directions:
1. Sprinkle chook wings with dry rub.
2. Place on a baking pan.
3. Set the Traeger wood pellet grill to 350 ranges F.
4. Preheat for 15 minutes even as the lid is closed.
5. Place the baking pan on the grill.
6. Cook for 50 mins.
7. Add butter to a pan over medium heat.
8. Sauté garlic for 3 minutes.
9. Stir in hot sauce and honey.
10. Cook for 5 minutes while stirring.
11. Coat the bird wings with the mixture.
12. Grill for 10 greater minutes.
Serving Suggestion: Serve with ranch

dressing.

Preparation / Cooking Tips: You could make the sauce earlier to lessen coaching time.

CAJUN CHICKEN

Preparation Time: 15 minutes
Cooking Time: 30 minutes Servings: 4

Ingredients:
2 lb. chicken wings
Poultry dry rub
Cajun seasoning
Directions:
1. Season the bird wings with the dry rub and Cajun seasoning.
2. Preheat the Traeger to 350 ranges F for 15 mins at the same time as the lid is closed.
3. Grill for 30 mins, flipping twice.
Serving Suggestion: Serve with vegetable aspect dish.
Preparation / Cooking Tips: You also can smoke the bird before grilling

CHILI BARBECUE CHICKEN

Preparation Time: 5 hours and 30 minutes
Cooking Time: 2 hours and 10 minutes
Servings: 4

Ingredients:
1 tablespoon brown sugar
1 tablespoon lime zest
1 tablespoon chili powder
1/2 teaspoon ground cumin
1/2 tablespoon ground espresso
Salt to taste

2 tablespoons olive oil
8 chicken legs
1/2 cup barbecue sauce
Directions:
1. Combine sugar, lime zest, chili powder, cumin, floor espresso and salt.
2. Drizzle the fowl legs with oil.
3. Sprinkle sugar combination all around the hen.
4. Cover with foil and refrigerate for 5 hours.
5. Set the Traeger timber pellet grill to 180 levels F.
6. Preheat it for 15 minutes even as the lid is closed.
7. Smoke the hen legs for 1 hour.
8. Increase temperature to 350 degrees F.
9. Grill the chook legs for another 1 hour, flipping once.
10. Brush the chook with barbeque sauce and grill for another 10 minutes.
Serving Suggestion: Garnish with chopped
parsley and lime wedges.
Preparation / Cooking Tips: You also can add chili powder to the fish fry sauce.

SERRANO CHICKEN WINGS

Preparation Time: 12 hours and 30 minutes
Cooking Time: 40 minutes Servings: 4

Ingredients:
4 lb. chicken wings
2 cups beer
2 teaspoons crushed red pepper
Cajun seasoning powder
1 lb. Serrano chili peppers

1 teaspoon fresh basil
1 teaspoon dried oregano
4 cloves garlic
1 cup vinegar
Salt and pepper to taste
Directions:
1. Soak the chook wings in beer.
2. Sprinkle with crushed crimson pepper.
3. Cover and refrigerate for 12 hours.
4. Remove chicken from brine.
5. Season with Cajun seasoning.
6. Preheat your Traeger wood pellet grill to 325 levels F for 15 mins whilst the lid is closed.
7. Add the hen wings and Serrano chili peppers at the grill.
8. Grill for five minutes according to aspect.
9. Remove chili peppers and area in a food processor.
10. Grill the chook for every other 20 minutes.
11. Add the rest of the ingredients to the meals processor.
12. Pulse until smooth.
13. Dip the hen wings in the sauce.
14. Grill for 5 mins and serve.
Serving Suggestion: Garnish with lemon wedges.
Preparation / Cooking Tips: You also can use organized pepper sauce to keep time.

SMOKED FRIED CHICKEN

Preparation Time: 1 hour and 30 minutes
Cooking Time: 3 hours Servings: 6

Ingredients:
lb. chicken
Vegetable oil

Salt and pepper to taste
2 tablespoons hot sauce
1-quart buttermilk
2 tablespoons brown sugar
1 tablespoon poultry dry rub
2 tablespoons onion powder
2 tablespoons garlic powder
2 1/2 cups all-purpose flour Peanut oil
Directions:
1. Set the Traeger wood pellet grill to 200 ranges F.
2. Preheat it for 15 minutes while the lid is closed.
3. Drizzle fowl with vegetable oil and sprinkle with salt and pepper.
4. Smoke chook for two hours and 30 minutes.
5. In a bowl, mix the new sauce, buttermilk and sugar.
6. Soak the smoked chook inside the aggregate.
7. Cover and refrigerate for 1 hour.
8. In some other bowl, blend the dry rub, onion powder, garlic powder and flour.
9. Coat the bird with the mixture.
10. Heat the peanut oil in a pan over medium heat.
11. Fry the chicken until golden and crispy.
Serving Suggestion: Serve with potato fries and ketchup.
Preparation / Cooking Tips: Drain bird on paper towels earlier than serving.

MAPLE TURKEY BREAST

Preparation Time: 4 hours and 30 minutes
Cooking Time: 2 hours
Servings: 4

Ingredients:

3 tablespoons olive oil
3 tablespoons dark brown sugar
3 tablespoons garlic, minced
2 tablespoons Cajun seasoning
2 tablespoons Worcestershire sauce
6 lb. turkey breast fillets
Directions:
1. Combine olive oil, sugar, garlic, Cajun seasoning and Worcestershire sauce in a bowl.
2. Soak the turkey breast fillets inside the marinade.
3. Cover and marinate for 4 hours.
4. Grill the turkey at 180 stages F for two hours.
Serving Suggestion: Let relaxation for 15 mins before serving.
Preparation / Cooking Tips: You can also sprinkle dry rub on the turkey before grilling.

CHICKEN TIKKA MASALA

Preparation Time: 12 hours and 40 minutes
Cooking Time: 1 hour
Servings: 4

Ingredients:
1 tablespoon garam masala
1 tablespoon smoked paprika
1 tablespoon ground coriander
1 tablespoon ground cumin
1 teaspoon ground cayenne pepper
1 teaspoon turmeric
1 onion, sliced
6 cloves garlic, minced
1/4 cup olive oil
1 tablespoon ginger, chopped

1 tablespoon lemon juice
1 1/2 cups Greek yogurt
1 tablespoon lime juice
1 tablespoon curry powder
Salt to taste
1 tablespoon lime juice
12 chicken drumsticks
Chopped cilantro

Directions:
1. Make the marinade by means of mixing all the spices, onion, garlic, olive oil, ginger, lemon juice, yogurt, lime juice, curry powder and salt.
2. Transfer to a food processor.
3. Pulse until smooth.
4. Divide the combination.
5. Marinade the bird inside the first bowl.
6. Cover the bowl and refrigerate for 12 hours.
7. Set the Traeger wooden pellet grill to high.
8. Preheat it for 15 mins at the same time as the lid is closed.
9. Grill the bird for 50 mins.
10. Garnish with the chopped cilantro.

Serving Suggestion: Serve with reserved sauce.

Preparation / Cooking Tips: You can also smoke the fowl earlier than grilling.

TURKEY WITH APRICOT BARBECUE GLAZE

Preparation Time: 30 minutes
Cooking Time: 30 minutes
Servings: 4

Ingredients:
4 turkey breast fillets
4 tablespoons chicken rub
1 cup apricot barbecue sauce

Directions:
1. Preheat the Traeger wooden pellet grill to 365 tiers F for 15 mins whilst the lid is closed.
2. Season the turkey fillets with the bird run.
3. Grill the turkey fillets for 5 mins according to aspect.
4. Brush each sides with the fish fry sauce and grill for some other 5 mins per facet.

Serving Suggestion: Serve with buttered cauliflower.

Preparation / Cooking Tips: You can sprinkle turkey with chili powder if you want your dish spicy.

TURKEY MEATBALLS

Preparation Time: 40 minutes
Cooking Time: 40 minutes **Servings:** 8

Ingredients:
1 1/4 lb. ground turkey
1/2 cup breadcrumbs
1 egg, beaten
1/4 cup milk
1 teaspoon onion powder
1/4 cup Worcestershire sauce
Pinch garlic salt
Salt and pepper to taste
1 cup cranberry jam
1/2 cup orange marmalade
1/2 cup chicken broth

Directions:
1. In a big bowl, mix the ground turkey, breadcrumbs, egg, milk, onion powder, Worcestershire sauce, garlic salt, salt and pepper.
2. Form meatballs from the combination.

3. three. Preheat the Traeger timber pellet grill to 350 tiers F for 15 minutes while the lid is closed.
4. Add the turkey meatballs to a baking pan.
5. Place the baking pan at the grill.
6. Cook for 20 minutes.
7. In a pan over medium heat, simmer the rest of the elements for 10 mins.
8. Add the grilled meatballs to the pan.
9. Coat with the aggregate.
10. Cook for 10 mins.

Serving Suggestion: Sprinkle meatballs with chopped parsley earlier than serving.

Preparation / Cooking Tips: You can upload chili powder to the meatball mixture if you need spicy flavor

GRILLED TUSCAN CHICKEN

Ingredients:
2 small handfuls of rosemary
125 ml of olive oil and more for the grill
the juice of 2 lemons
salt and grounded pepper
2 whole chickens
3 handfuls of rocket lemon wedges

Directions:
1. Set up the grill for medium-high heat.
2. Mix the rosemary, the olive oil, lemon juice, the salt and floor pepper in a resalable plastic bag.
3. Cut the hen in half of lengthwise, the usage of kitchen scissors and put off the backbone. Put it into the resalable bag with the marinade.
4. Clean and oil the grate. Take off the chicken from the marinade and placed it on the grill, skin-aspect down.

5. Press the chicken using two foil-protected bricks and grill for 20 mins.
6. Turn and hold cooking for an additional 1520 mins.
7. Move onto a reducing board and allow it rest for five minutes earlier than carving it.
8. Serve on a bed of rocket and with lemon wedges nearby.

FISH AND SEAFOOD RECIPES

SMOKED SHRIMP

Preparation Time: 4 hours and 15 minutes
Cooking Time: 10 minutes
Servings: 4

Ingredients:
4 tablespoons olive oil
1 tablespoon Cajun seasoning
2 cloves garlic, minced
1 tablespoon lemon juice
Salt to taste
2 lb. shrimp, peeled and deveined

Directions:
1. Combine all of the substances in a sealable plastic bag.
2. Toss to coat evenly.
3. Marinate within the refrigerator for four hours.
4. four. Set the Traeger wood pellet grill to excessive.
5. Preheat it for 15 mins whilst the lid is closed.
6. Thread shrimp onto skewers.
7. Grill for four minutes according to side.

Serving Suggestion: Garnish with lemon wedges.

Preparation / Cooking Tips: Soak skewers first in water if you are using wood skewers.

COD WITH LEMON HERB BUTTER

Preparation Time: 30 minutes
Cooking Time: 15 minutes
Servings: 4

Ingredients:
4 tablespoons butter
1 clove garlic, minced
1 tablespoon tarragon, chopped
1 tablespoon lemon juice
1 teaspoon lemon zest
Salt and pepper to taste
1 lb. cod fillet

Directions:
1. Preheat the Traeger wood pellet grill to excessive for 15 mins whilst the lid is closed.
2. In a bowl, mix the butter, garlic, tarragon, lemon juice and lemon zest, salt and pepper.
3. Place the fish in a baking pan.
4. four. Spread the butter combination on top.
5. Bake the fish for 15 minutes.

Serving Suggestion: Spoon sauce over the fish earlier than serving.

Preparation / Cooking Tips: You also can use different white fish fillet for this recipe.

SALMON WITH AVOCADO SALSA

Preparation Time: 30 minutes

Cooking Time: 20 minutes
Servings: 6

Ingredients:
3 lb. salmon fillet
Garlic salt and pepper to taste
4 cups avocado, sliced into cubes
1 onion, chopped
1 jalapeño pepper, minced
1 tablespoon lime juice
1 tablespoon olive oil
¼ cup cilantro, chopped Salt to taste

Directions:
1. Sprinkle both aspects of salmon with garlic salt and pepper.
2. Set the Traeger timber pellet grill to smoke.
3. Grill the salmon for 7 to 8 mins per facet.
4. While waiting, prepare the salsa via combining the remaining components in a bowl.
5. Serve salmon with the avocado salsa.
6. Serving Suggestion: Garnish with lemon wedges.

Preparation / Cooking Tips: You can also use tomato salsa for this recipe if you don't have avocados.

BUTTERED CRAB LEGS

Preparation Time: 30 minutes
Cooking Time: 10 minutes
Servings: 4

Ingredients:
12 tablespoons butter
1 tablespoon parsley, chopped
1 tablespoon tarragon, chopped
1 tablespoon chives, chopped

1 tablespoon lemon juice
4 lb. king crab legs, split in the center
Directions:
1. Set the Traeger wooden pellet grill to 375 stages F.
2. Preheat it for 15 minutes whilst lid is closed.
3. In a pan over medium warmth, simmer the butter, herbs and lemon juice for 2 mins.
4. Place the crab legs on the grill.
5. Pour half of the sauce on top.
6. Grill for 10 mins.
7. Serve with the reserved butter sauce.
Serving Suggestion: Garnish with lemon wedges.
Preparation / Cooking Tips: You also can use shrimp for this recipe.

GRILLED BLACKENED SALMON

Preparation Time: 15 minutes
Cooking Time: 30 minutes Servings: 4

Ingredients:
4 salmon fillet
Blackened dry rub
Italian seasoning powder
Directions:
1. Season salmon fillets with dry rub and seasoning powder.
2. Grill in the Traeger timber pellet grill at 325 degrees F for 10 to 15 mins in step with aspect.
Serving Suggestion: Garnish with lemon wedges.
Preparation / Cooking Tips: You also can drizzle salmon with lemon juice.

SPICY SHRIMP

Preparation Time: 45 minutes
Cooking Time: 10 minutes
Servings: 4

Ingredients:
3 tablespoons olive oil
6 cloves garlic
2 tablespoons chicken dry rub
6 oz. chili
1 1/2 tablespoons white vinegar
1 1/2 teaspoons sugar
2 lb. shrimp, peeled and deveined
Directions:
1. Add olive oil, garlic, dry rub, chili, vinegar and sugar in a food processor.
2. Blend until smooth.
3. Transfer aggregate to a bowl.
4. Stir in shrimp.
5. Cover and refrigerate for 30 mins.
6. Preheat the Traeger timber pellet grill to hit for 15 minutes whilst the lid is closed.
7. Thread shrimp onto skewers.
8. Grill for three minute consistent with facet.
Serving Suggestion: Garnish with chopped herbs.
Preparation / Cooking Tips: You also can upload vegetables to the skewers.

GRILLED HERBED TUNA

Preparation Time: 4 hours and 15 minutes
Cooking Time: 10 minutes
Servings: 6

Ingredients:
6 tuna steaks
1 tablespoon lemon zest

1 tablespoon fresh thyme, chopped
1 tablespoon fresh parsley, chopped Garlic salt to taste

Directions:
1. Sprinkle the tuna steaks with lemon zest, herbs and garlic salt.
2. Cover with foil.
3. Refrigerate for 4 hours.
4. Grill for 3 mins according to side.

Serving Suggestion: Top with lemon slices earlier than serving.

Preparation / Cooking Tips: Take the fish out of the fridge 30 mins before cooking.

ROASTED SNAPPER

Preparation Time: 30 minutes
Cooking Time: 15 minutes
Servings: 4

Ingredients:
4 snapper fillets
Salt and pepper to taste
2 teaspoons dried tarragon
Olive oil
2 lemons, sliced

Directions:
1. Set the Traeger wood pellet grill to high.
2. Preheat it for 15 minutes at the same time as the lid is closed.
3. Add 1 fish fillet on pinnacle of a foil sheet.
4. Sprinkle with salt, pepper and tarragon.
5. Drizzle with oil.
6. Place lemon slices on pinnacle.
7. Fold and seal the packets.
8. Put the foil packets at the grill.
9. Bake for 15 minutes.
10. Open cautiously and serve.

Serving Suggestion: Drizzle with melted butter earlier than serving.

Preparation / Cooking Tips: You also can upload asparagus spears or broccoli in the packet to prepare dinner with the fish.

FISH FILLETS WITH PESTO

Preparation Time: 15 minutes
Cooking Time: 15 minutes

Ingredients:
2 cups fresh basil
1 cup parsley, chopped
1/2 cup walnuts
1/2 cup olive oil
1 cup Parmesan cheese, grated
Salt and pepper to taste
4 white fish fillets

Directions:
1. Preheat the Traeger wood pellet grill to excessive for 15 minutes at the same time as the lid is closed.
2. Add all of the substances besides fish to a meals processor.
3. Pulse until smooth. Set aside.
4. Season fish with salt and pepper.
5. Grill for six to 7 minutes consistent with facet.
6. Serve with the pesto sauce.

Serving Suggestion: Garnish with clean basil leaves.

Preparation / Cooking Tips: You can also unfold a little bit of the pesto at the fish before grilling.

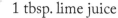

HALIBUT WITH GARLIC PESTO

Preparation Time: 20 minutes
Cooking Time: 10 minutes Servings: 4

Ingredients:
4 halibut fillets
1 cup olive oil
Salt and pepper to taste
1/4 cup garlic, chopped
1/4 cup pine nuts
Directions:
1. Set the Traeger timber pellet grill to smoke.
2. Establish fire for 5 minutes.
3. Set temperature to high.
4. four. Place a forged iron on a grill.
5. Season fish with salt and pepper.
6. Add fish to the pan.
7. Drizzle with a touch oil.
8. Sear for four minutes consistent with aspect.
9. Prepare the garlic pesto by pulsing the ultimate substances in the food processor until smooth.
10. Serve fish with garlic pesto.
Serving Suggestion: Sprinkle with fresh herbs before serving.
Preparation / Cooking Tips: You also can use other white fish fillets for this recipe.

GRILLED SHRIMP WITH APPLE AND CHARRED SCALLIONS

Ingredients:
1/4 cup and 2 1/2 tbsp. of extra virgin olive oil
1 tbsp. sherry vinegar
1 tbsp. lime juice
1/2 tsp sweet smoked paprika
1/2 tsp Dijon mustard salt and grounded pepper
6 scallions
1-pound medium shrimp, shelled and deveined
1 Granny Smith apple—peeled, cored and julienned
1 tbsp. of toasted sesame seeds
Directions:
1. In a touch bowl, mix1/four cup of the olive oil with the vinegar, the lime juice, paprika, and mustard. Season the dressing with salt and grounded pepper. In a big pot with salted bubbling water, wince the scallions until vibrant green, around 1 minute. Drain the scallions, wash underneath cold water, and pat them dry.
2. Set up the grill. Rub the scallions with half tbsp. of the olive oil, then season with salt and level-headed pepper. In a bowl, blend the shrimp with the closing tbsp. of olive oil and season with salt and level-headed pepper. Grill the scallions over high warmness till gently singed, round 30 seconds for each aspect. Grill the shrimp till lightly singed and white all through, around 1 minute for every side.
3. In some other bowl, mix the apple with 1 tbsp. of the dressing. Cut the grilled scallions into 2inch lengths. Put the scallions and apple on a platter and place the shrimp on top. Shower the rest of the dressing over the shrimp, sprinkle with the sesame seeds and serve.

SHRIMP AND SCALLOPS WITH LEMONY SOY

Ingredients:
1 1/2 cups low-sodium soy sauce
1 cup of mirin
1cup sake
2 sliced lemons
2 sliced jalapeños
1-pound medium shrimp, shelled and deveined
1-pound large sea scallops' vegetable oil for the grill

Directions:
1. In a tumbler bowl, mix the soy sauce with the mirin, sake, lemon slices, and jalapeños.
2. String the shrimp onto 8 bamboo skewers and upload them to the marinade, then cover. Repeat with the scallops. Refrigerate the fish for 30 mins, turning as soon as.
3. Set up the grill and oil the grates. Spoon the shrimp and scallops with oil and grill over excessive heat, turning on multiple occasion, till gently singed, around four minutes. Serve straight away.

SHRIMP AND LEMON SKEWERS WITH FETA DILL SAUCE

Ingredients:
1/2 cup plain low-fat yogurt
1 thinly sliced scallion (white and light green parts only)
4 finely chopped large garlic cloves
2 1/2 tbsp. of finely chopped dill
1/2 cup crumbled Feta cheese
salt and grounded pepper

1/4 cup of extra virgin olive oil
2 pounds peeled and deveined large shrimp
2 lemons, each cut into 12 wedges

Directions:
1. Set up the grill. In a medium bowl, mix the yogurt with the scallion, 1/4 of the garlic, and 1/2 tbsp. of the dill. Add within the Feta, crushing it. Season with salt and level-headed pepper.
2. In a large bowl, mix the last minced garlic and 2 tbsp. of dill with the olive oil. Add the shrimp and the lemons, season with salt and grounded pepper, then cover. String four shrimp and 2 lemon wedges onto 12 skewers. Season with salt and grounded pepper and grill over a medium-hot warmth, turning once in a while, till the shrimp are singed and cooked through around 5 mins. Move the skewers onto a platter and serve without a second's put off with the Feta sauce.

SHRIMP AND CHORIZO MIXED GRILL

Ingredients:
For the Cilantro Sour Cream Sauce
1 1/4 cups of sour cream
1 cup cilantro leaves
1/4 cup of mayonnaise
1 small sliced jalapeno
2 tbsp. of fresh lime juice
1 1/4 tbsp. of Kosher salt
For the Dressing
5 tbsp. of extra virgin olive oil
1/4 cup of fresh lime juice
1 finely grated garlic clove
2 tbsp. of finely chopped cilantro
1 tsp of honey
1 tsp of Kosher salt

For Grilling and Assembly
1 1/2 lb. of jumbo or large shrimp, peeled and deveined
1/2 tsp of chili powder
1 1/4 tsp of Kosher salt
1 green cabbage, cut in 4 wedges
6 links of fresh chorizo sausage canola oil
2 bunches of medium asparagus lime wedges

Directions:
1. Set up the grill for 2 zone heat.
2. Mix the sour cream, the cilantro, mayonnaise, the jalapeno, lime juice, and salt in a blender and chill.
3. Mix the oil, lime juice, the garlic, cilantro, the honey, and the salt in a big bowl.
4. Mix the shrimp, the chili powder, and 1 tsp of salt in a medium bowl.
5. Grill the cabbage over direct heat, turning as soon as in a whilst, until crisp, around 20 mins. Move onto a reducing board and allow it cool.
6. In the meantime, grill the sausages over indirect warmth, regularly turning, until cooked through, around 15 minutes. Move onto a platter and cover.
7. Oil the grate and grill the asparagus, till lightly singed and cooked via then flow onto the platter with sausages.
8. Slice the cabbage wedges in lengthy strips and blend with the dressing. Season with salt and pass onto the platter.
9. Serve with lime wedges and bitter cream sauce nearby.

GRILLED SHRIMP WITH MISO BUTTER

Ingredients:
1 stick of softened unsalted butter
2 tbsp. white miso
1/2 tsp finely grated lemon zest
1 tbsp. fresh lemon juice
1 tbsp. thinly sliced scallion and more for the garnish
1 pound shelled and deveined large shrimp
2 tbsp. of canola oil
1 large minced garlic clove
1 tsp Korean chili powder (gochujang) or any other chili powder 1 tsp Kosher salt
1 1/2 tsp pickled mustard seeds in brine

Directions:
1. In a blender, blend the butter with the miso, the lemon zest, and lemon juice and blend it till smooth. Add the tbsp. of scallion and blend it once more. Put the miso butter into a large bowl and positioned aside.
2. In any other large bowl, mix the shrimp with the oil, the garlic, chili powder, and salt and let it relaxation for 10 mins.
3. Set up the grill. Grill the shrimps over excessive heat, turning once, till cooked through, around 4 mins. Promptly add the shrimp to the miso butter and blend until well covered. Top the shrimp with scallions and the mustard seeds and serve.

GRILLED SALMON WITH MEYER LEMONS AND CREAMY CUCUMBER SALAD

Ingredients:
Salmon:

4 (6ounce) skin-on wild salmon fillets
1/2 cup extra virgin olive oil and more for
the grilling
1 tbsp. grated Meyer or regular lemon zest
the juice of 2 Meyer or regular lemons and
1 or 2 Meyer or regular lemons, sliced into
8 thin rounds
1 tbsp. of minced fresh dill
1 tbsp. of pink or regular sea salt
<u>Creamy Cucumber Salad:</u>
1/2 cup mayonnaise (preferably
Hellmann's)
1/2 cup of sour cream
1 tbsp. fresh Meyer or regular lemon juice
1 tsp minced fresh dill
1 tsp sea salt
1/2 tsp of grounded black pepper
2 English cucumbers, peeled, halved and
cut into
1/4inch dice
<u>Garnish:</u>
1 tbsp. of minced chives
Directions:
To put together the salmon:
1. Spoon the pores and skin side of the
salmon fillets with some olive oil. In a bit
bowl, mix the half cup olive oil, the lemon
zest, lemon juice, dill, and the salt. Empty
the mixture right into a dish and placed the
fillets pores and skin facet up. Cover and
refrigerate for 60 minutes.
2. In the meantime, put together the
creamy cucumber salad. In a medium bowl,
blend collectively the mayonnaise, the sour
cream, lemon juice, dill, the salt, and the
grounded pepper. Wrap in the cucumber
till absolutely covered. Taste and add the
lemon juice or salt if necessary. Cover and
refrigerate for no more than hours.
3. Set up the grill to a medium-hot

warmness and oil the grate.
4. Put the fillets skin side down at the
grill and spoon them with the marinade.
Cover the grill and keep cooking without
flipping until the salmon drops about 10 to
12 minutes. Spoon the lemon slices on the
two sides with oil and grill till marks show
up, 1 to 2 mins for each facet.
5. Place the fish onto plates or on a serving
platter. Put 1 or 2 grilled lemon slices over
each fillet and sprinkle with chives. To be
served with the cucumber salad.
6. Store the ultimate salmon and cucumber
salad inside the cooler for no extra than
days.

SWORDFISH STEAKS WITH OLIVE GREMOLATA

Ingredients:
7 tbsp. of olive oil and more for the grill
3/4 cup of torn fresh breadcrumbs
Kosher salt and grounded pepper
2 tbsp. of chopped fresh parsley
2 tbsp. coarsely chopped green olives
(Castelvetrano)
1 tbsp. coarsely chopped golden raisins
2 tsp of finely grated lemon zest
2 (8–10ounce) swordfish steaks (1–1 1/4"
thick) lemon wedges.
Directions:
1. Set up the grill for medium-high
warmth and oil the grate. Put the
breadcrumbs with 1 tbsp. of oil in a bowl,
then season with salt and level-headed
pepper. Put a cast-iron skillet at the grill
and toast breadcrumbs, turning as soon as
in a while, until browned, round five
minutes. Move the toasted breadcrumbs
into a bowl and permit cool.

2. Add parsley, olives, the raisins, lemon zest, and 5 tbsp. oil to breadcrumbs and mix. Put the gremolata aside.

3. Spoon the swordfish with the remaining tbsp. of oil, then season with salt and level-headed pepper. Grill until is softly singed and cooked thru (fish will sense firm, like a cooked red meat chop), about 6–8 mins for every aspect. Move the swordfish onto a platter and pinnacle with gremolata. Present with lemon wedges.

VEGETABLE RECIPES

KALE CHIPS

Preparation Time: 30 minutes
Cooking Time: 20 minutes
Servings: 4

Ingredients:
4 cups kale leaves
Olive oil
Salt to taste
Directions:
1. Drizzle kale with oil and season with salt.
2. Set the Traeger wood pellet grill to 250 levels F.
3. Preheat it for 15 minutes at the same time as the lid is closed.
4. Add the kale leaves to a baking pan.
5. Place the pan on the grill.
6. Cook the kale for 20 minutes or until crispy.
Serving Suggestion: Serve with garlic mayo dip.

Preparation / Cooking Tips: Store in an airtight jar with lid for up to three days.

SWEET POTATO FRIES

Preparation Time: 30 minutes
Cooking Time: 40 minutes
Servings: 4

Ingredients:
sweet potatoes, sliced into strips
tablespoons olive oil
2 tablespoons fresh rosemary, chopped
Salt and pepper to taste
Directions:
1. Set the Traeger timber pellet grill to 450 tiers F.
2. Preheat it for 10 minutes.
3. Spread the sweet potato strips within the baking pan.
4. Toss in olive oil and sprinkle with rosemary, salt and pepper.
5. Cook for 15 mins.
6. Flip and cook dinner for every other 15 mins.
7. Flip and cook dinner for 10 more mins.
Serving Suggestion: Serve with mayo or ketchup.
Preparation13
/ Cooking Tips: Soak sweet potatoes in water before cooking to prevent browning.

POTATO FRIES WITH CHIPOTLE PEPPERS

Preparation Time: 30 minutes
Cooking Time: 30 minutes
Servings: 4

4 potatoes, sliced into strips
3 tablespoons olive oil
Salt and pepper to taste
1 cup mayonnaise
2 chipotle peppers in adobo sauce
2 tablespoons lime juice
Directions:
1. 1. Set the Traeger timber pellet grill to high.
2. Preheat it for 15 minutes at the same time as the lid is closed.
3. Coat the potato strips with oil.
4. Sprinkle with salt and pepper.
5. Put a baking pan on the grate.
6. Transfer potato strips to the pan.
7. Cook potatoes until crispy.
8. Mix the final components.
9. Pulse in a meals processor till pureed.
10. Serve potato fries with chipotle dip.
Serving Suggestion: Sprinkle with pepper before serving.
Preparation / Cooking Tips: You can also use sweet potatoes as opposed to potatoes.

GRILLED ZUCCHINI

Preparation Time: 30 minutes
Cooking Time: 30 minutes
Servings: 4

Ingredients:
4 zucchinis, sliced into strips
1 tablespoon sherry vinegar
2 tablespoons olive oil
Salt and pepper to taste
2 fresh thymes, chopped
Directions:
1. Place the zucchini strips in a bowl.
2. Mix the remaining components and pour into the zucchini.

3. Coat evenly.
4. Set the Traeger wooden pellet grill to 350 degrees F.
5. Preheat for 15 minutes even as the lid is closed.
6. Place the zucchini at the grill.
7. Cook for 3 minutes per facet.
Serving Suggestion: Serve with your favorite dipping sauce.
Preparation / Cooking Tips: Wait for grill marks to appear earlier than flipping.

SMOKED POTATO SALAD

Preparation Time: 1 hour and 15 minutes
Cooking Time: 40 minutes Servings: 4

Ingredients:
2 lb. potatoes
2 tablespoons olive oil
2 cups mayonnaise
1 tablespoon white wine vinegar
1 tablespoon dry mustard
1/2 onion, chopped
2 celery stalks, chopped
Salt and pepper to taste
Directions:
1. Coat the potatoes with oil.
2. Smoke the potatoes inside the Traeger wood pellet grill at 180 stages F for 20 mins.
3. Increase temperature to 450 degrees F and prepare dinner for 20 extra mins.
4. Transfer to a bowl and let cool.
5. Peel potatoes.
6. Slice into cubes.
7. Refrigerate for 30 minutes.
8. Stir within the rest of the ingredients.
Serving Suggestion: Garnish with chopped chives.

Preparation / Cooking Tips: You also can upload chopped hard-boiled eggs to the combination.

BAKED PARMESAN MUSHROOMS

Preparation Time: 15 minutes
Cooking Time: 15 minutes
Servings: 8

Ingredients:
8 mushroom caps
1/2 cup Parmesan cheese, grated
1/2 teaspoon garlic salt
1/4 cup mayonnaise
Pinch paprika Hot sauce
Directions:
1. Place mushroom caps in a baking pan.
2. Mix the final elements in a bowl.
3. Scoop the combination onto the mushroom.
4. Place the baking pan at the grill.
5. Cook inside the Traeger timber pellet grill at 350 levels F for 15 mins while the lid is closed.
Serving Suggestion: Garnish with chopped herbs before serving.
Preparation / Cooking Tips: You can also upload chopped sausage to the combination.

ROASTED SPICY TOMATOES

Preparation Time: 30 minutes
Cooking Time: 1 hour and 30 minutes
Servings: 4

Ingredients:

Ingredients:
2 lb. large tomatoes, sliced in half
Olive oil
2 tablespoons garlic, chopped
3 tablespoons parsley, chopped
Salt and pepper to taste Hot pepper sauce
Directions:
1. Set the temperature to 400 stages F.
2. Preheat it for 15 mins even as the lid is closed.
3. Add tomatoes to a baking pan.
4. Drizzle with oil and sprinkle with garlic, parsley, salt and pepper.
5. Roast for 1 hour and 30 mins.
6. Drizzle with warm pepper sauce and serve.
Serving Suggestion: Serve as side dish to a major course.
Preparation / Cooking Tips: You can also puree the roasted tomatoes and use as sauce for pasta or as dip for chips.

GRILLED CORN WITH HONEY & BUTTER

Preparation Time: 30 minutes
Cooking Time: 10 minutes
Servings: 4

Ingredients:
6 pieces of corn
2 tablespoons olive oil
1/2 cup butter
1/2 cup honey
1 tablespoon smoked salt Pepper to taste
Directions:
1. Preheat the timber pellet grill to excessive for 15 minutes while the lid is closed.

2. Brush the corn with oil and butter.
3. Grill the corn for 10 mins, turning from time to time.
4. Mix honey and butter.
5. Brush corn with this aggregate and sprinkle with smoked salt and pepper.
Serving Suggestion: Serve with additional honey butter dip.
Preparation / Cooking Tips: Slice off the kernels and serve as facet dish to a chief course.

GRILLED SWEET POTATO PLANKS

Preparation Time: 30 minutes
Cooking Time: 30 minutes
Servings: 8

Ingredients:
5 sweet potatoes, sliced into planks
1 tablespoon olive oil
1 teaspoon onion powder
Salt and pepper to taste
Directions:
1. Set the Traeger wooden pellet grill to excessive.
2. Preheat it for 15 mins whilst the lid is closed.
3. Coat the candy potatoes with oil.
4. Sprinkle with onion powder, salt and pepper.
5. Grill the candy potatoes for 15 minutes.
Serving Suggestion: Serve with garlic mayo dip or your favorite dip.
Preparation / Cooking Tips: Grill for a few more mins if you want your candy potatoes crispier.

ROASTED VEGGIES & HUMMUS

Preparation Time: 30 minutes
Cooking Time: 20 minutes
Servings: 4

Ingredients:
1 white onion, sliced into wedges
2 cups butternut squash
2 cups cauliflower, sliced into florets
1 cup mushroom buttons
Olive oil
Salt and pepper to taste
Hummus
Directions:
1. Set the Traeger wood pellet grill to excessive.
2. Preheat it for 10 mins even as the lid is closed.
3. Add the greens to a baking pan.
4. Roast for 20 minutes.
5. Serve roasted greens with hummus.
Serving Suggestion: Serve as appetizer.
Preparation / Cooking Tips: You can also spread a little hummus at the vegetables earlier than roasting.

GRILLED SQUID SALAD WITH ARUGULA AND MELON

Ingredients:
1 pound cleaned baby squid
1/2 tsp finely grated lemon zest
1/2 tsp finely grated lime zest
1/2 tsp finely grated orange zest
1 1/4 tsp of crushed red pepper
1 cup of extra virgin olive oil
2 cups of coarsely chopped parsley leaves

6 anchovy fillets
4 large smashed garlic cloves
2 tbsp. drained capers
1 large shallot, chopped
2 tbsp. of red wine vinegar sea salt and grounded black pepper
2 tbsp. fresh lemon juice
4 ounces' baby arugula
3 cups cantaloupe cubes
2 inner celery ribs, thinly sliced
1 thinly sliced small hot red chili

Directions:

1. Slash the squid our bodies the long way and open them on a work floor. Score a crosscut design at the internal parts and circulate right into a bowl. Add in the tentacles, the lemon zest, the lime zest, and the orange zest and a tsp of the crushed crimson pepper and 1/four cup of the olive oil. Refrigerate for 60 minutes. In the meantime, in a blender, put the parsley, anchovies, the garlic, escapades, and shallot and mix until finely slashed. Add in 1/2 cup of the olive oil and blend till puree forms. Add the vinegar and the final 1/four teaspoon of beaten crimson pepper and season the salsa Verde with salt and grounded pepper.

2. Set up the grill or preheat a grill pan. Season the squid with salt. Grill over high warmth, turning as soon as till singed in spots, round five mins. Move all of the squid our bodies to a work surface and slice them. Move the squid right into a medium bowl and mix with 1/2 of the salsa Verde.

3. In a massive bowl, mix the last 1/4 cup of olive oil with the lemon squeeze, then season with salt. Add the arugula, melon, the celery, and crimson warm chili and mingle delicately. Add the squid and

mingle once extra. Move the salad onto a platter or into plates and serve with the relaxation of the salsa Verde nearby.

GREEK GRILLED SCALLOP SANDWICHES

Ingredients:
1/4 cup Greek-style whole-milk yogurt
1 pinch of crumbled saffron threads
1½ tsp of rice vinegar sea salt and grounded pepper
1 thinly sliced black plum
extra virgin olive oil
12 large sea scallops
2 thin slices of prosciutto, cut into strips
36 pea tendrils (1 cup)

Directions:

1. Set up the grill. In a bowl, mix the yogurt, saffron, and the vinegar, then season with salt and level-headed pepper.

2. Spoon the plum slices with oil and grill over excessive warmness until delicately roasted, about 30 seconds for each aspect. Spoon the scallops with oil, season with salt and pepper, and grill them over high heat till singed and cooked through, around 1/2 minutes for every facet.

3. Cut every scallop in halves. Place a plum slice on the bottom portion of each scallop. Lay the prosciutto strips over the plums. At that point, top each one with 2 pea tendrils and cowl with the scallop. Secure the use of toothpicks and vicinity 3 on each plate. Top every scallop sandwich with a tsp of the yogurt sauce and with the relaxation of the pea tendrils. Shower with olive oil, sprinkle with salt, and serve.

EASY GRILLED PAELLA

Ingredients:
3 cups fish stock or chicken broth
1/2 pound of deveined large shrimp, shells reserved
1 pinch of saffron threads, crumbled
1/2 lemon
2 tbsp. of extra virgin olive oil
6 ounces of fresh chorizo sliced
1/2 inch thick
2 finely chopped ripe tomatoes
2 minced garlic cloves
1 tsp of smoked paprika
1 1/2 cups of Calasparra or Arborio rice (10 ounces)
1/2 pound cleaned halved squid bodies, scored in a crosshatch pattern and cut into 2inch pieces
1 pound of scrubbed cockles
1/2-pound jumbo lump crab
1 cup of roasted red peppers, cut into strips
2 tbsp. of chopped parsley
Hot sauce and lemon wedges

Directions:
1. In a huge skillet, mix the inventory with the shrimp shells and saffron. Crush inside the lemon, add water until the half of the skillet, and produce to a stew. Take far from the warmth and permit it sit down for 10 mins. Strain the soup and eliminate the solids.
2. In the meantime, set up the grill for high warmness. Place a huge flameproof skillet at the grill and heat the olive oil in it. Add the chorizo and cover the skillet. Cook until the chorizo is sizzling and gently browned, round 5 minutes. Add the tomatoes, garlic and the smoked paprika, then cowl the skillet, and hold cooking, turning a few times, until the tomatoes are mellowed- around five mins. Add the rice and mix to cowl all with the tomato mixture. Add within the shrimp juices. Cover the skillet and preserve cooking till half of the soup has been reduced- round 10 minutes. Add within the shrimp, squid, and the cockles. Cover the skillet and maintain cooking till the rice is al dente, and the fish is cooked, round 8 mins. Add within the crab, the peppers, and parsley and prepare dinner just until warmed through. Serve with warm sauce and lemon wedges.

SPICED CRAB TACOS

Ingredients:
2 finely chopped medium tomatoes
2 large red radishes, cut into dice
1/2 finely chopped small red onion
1/4 cup chopped cilantro
2 tsp of Sriracha chili sauce
salt
1 large jalapeño
1/2 diced red bell pepper
1/2 diced yellow bell pepper
3 tbsp. of extra virgin olive oil
1 tbsp. fresh lime juice
1 tbsp. of chopped mint
1/2-pound lump crabmeat
8-10-inch flour tortillas, halved or quartered

Directions:
1. In a medium bowl, mix the tomatoes, radishes, the crimson onion, 2 tbsp. of the cilantro, and the Sriracha sauce. Season the salsa with salt.
2. Set up the grill or preheat a grill pan. Grill the jalapeño pepper over mild

warmness, turning as soon as or twice till singed everywhere. Let it cool after which cast off the scorched skin, stem, and seeds. Finely hack the jalapeño. In some other medium bowl, blend the jalapeño, the crimson and yellow bell peppers, the olive oil, lime juice, the mint, and the final 2 tbsp. of cilantro. Delicately bend within the crabmeat and season with salt.

3. Grill the tortillas over high warmth till singed in spots, round 20 seconds for every facet. Serve the spiced crab with the nice and cozy tortillas and salsa.

GRILLED VEGGIES WITH MUSTARD VINAIGRETTE

Ingredients:
1/4 cup red wine vinegar
1 tbsp Dijon mustard
1 tbsp. honey
1/2 tsp salt
1/8 tsp pepper
1/4 cup canola oil 1/4 cup olive oil
Vegetables:
2 large sweet onions
2 medium zucchini
2 yellow summer squash
2 large halved and seeded sweet red peppers
1 bunch green onions, trimmed cooking spray

Directions:
1. In a bit bowl, mix the initial five fixings. Continuously upload in oils till all mixed.
2. Strip and quarter each sweet onion. Cut the zucchini and the yellow squash lengthwise into 1/2inches thick slices. Spray the onions, zucchini, yellow squash, and remaining greens with cooking spray

on all sides.

3. Grill the candy onions over medium warmth for 1520 minutes, turning occasionally. Grill the zucchini, squash, and peppers over medium warmness for 1015 minutes or till gently seared, turning once. Grill the green onions for twenty-four minutes or until softly singed, turning once.

4. Cut the vegetables into pieces and area them in a bowl. Add half of cup vinaigrette. Serve with vinaigrette nearby way of.

GRILLED BRUSSELS SPROUTS

Ingredients:
16 fresh trimmed Brussels sprouts
1 sweet red pepper
1 medium onion
1/2 tsp salt
1/2 tsp of garlic powder
1/4 tsp grounded pepper
1 tbsp. of olive oil

Directions:
1. In a huge pot, warmness the water to the point of boiling. Add the Brussels sprouts in. Decrease the warmth and steam for 4 or 6 mins. Let it cool and cut every piece down the middle.

2. Cut the pink pepper and onion into 11/2inch portions. String them along with the Brussels sprouts on four metallic or drenched timber skewers. Add the garlic powder and the grounded pepper. Spoon the greens with oil, add the salt and blend again. Grill them over medium heat or till veggies are tender, about 1012 mins, turning occasionally.

HORSERADISH-CRUSTED STANDING RIB ROAST WITH PAN GRAVY

Servings: 6 to 8

Few foods are as impressive as a standing rib roast—it's perfect for holidays and special occasions. I've taken its normal accompaniment, horseradish, and used it in a flavor paste that will turn into a tasty crust,giving the roast a smoky bite. Make sure you follow my method exactly; do it, and you'll be rewarded with a delicious, succulent roast. You can only use this method with a kamado grill because of its superior heat retention. And I'm serious— do not peek. If you open the dome midway through, all is lost. This would be a good time to invest in a probe thermometer if you have not done so already, which will allow you to monitor the roast's internal temperature without lifting the dome.

Ingredients:

1 (5- to 6-pound) bone-in standing rib roast, trimmed of excess fat 6 large cloves garlic, peeled
1 cup grated, peeled fresh horseradish or well-drained prepared horseradish
2 tablespoons chopped fresh oregano 1 tablespoon chopped fresh rosemary 1 tablespoon kosher salt
1 tablespoon freshly ground black pepper y cup extra-virgin olive oil M cup dry white wine

1 tablespoon gravy flour or all-purpose flour
2 cups low-sodium chicken broth 2 sprigs fresh thyme
½ cup (M stick) unsalted butter, reduce into tablespoons

Directions:

1. Light a hearth within the kamado grill using your favored method. After about 10 minutes, region the grill rack in position, close the dome, and open the higher and lower dampers all of the way. When the temperature reaches 500° F, alter the dampers to preserve the temperature.
2. Place the roasting pan at the grill, near the dome, and roast at 450° to 500° F for forty-five mins.
3. Adjust the dampers to drop the grill temperature to 350° F and roast for another 30 minutes.
4. Close the dampers completely and allow the roast cook till it has an inner temperature of 125° to 130° F. Depending on the tightness of your seal, this will take anywhere from 30 to 70 minutes. No peeking! Trust your kamado grill. The key to fulfillment is the internal temperature. As quickly as you hit it, take away the roast from the grill.
5. Transfer the roast to a slicing board, loosely tent with aluminum foil, and let relaxation for 20 to 30 mins. The inner temperature will upward thrust 5 to 10 degrees. Meanwhile, pour off a number of the fats and location the pan over burners at the range set at medium heat. Pour inside the wine and scrape up the browned bits from the bottom of the pan. Whisk within the flour, then whisk inside the broth and upload the thyme. Cook, stirring

till the gravy reaches the thickness you like. Remove the pan from the heat and whisk inside the butter. Carve meat into slices and serve with the pan gravy.

GRILLED CLAMS WITH HERB BUTTER

Ingredients:
1/2 cup (1 stick) unsalted butter
1 tbsp. chopped flat leaf parsley
1 tbsp. of chopped fresh dill
1 tbsp. of chopped scallion
1 tbsp. of fresh lemon juice
Kosher salt and grounded black pepper
24 scrubbed littlenecks clams
lemon wedges

Directions:
1. Blend the first five fixings in a medium bowl. Season it with salt and black pepper.
2. Set up the grill for medium-hot heat, or heat a gas grill to excessive. Place the clams at the rack and close the lid. Grill till the clams open, approximately 68 mins (eliminate people who don't open). Use tongs to move onto a platter, being cautious to keep as lots clam juice as possible.
3. Sprinkle the clams with herb butter and hold cooking till the butter softens.
4. Serve heat with lemon wedges nearby.

FLOUNDER WITH CORN AND TASSO MAQUE CHOUX

Ingredients:
4 1/4inchthick shallot slices, divided
4 tbsp. (1/2 stick) unsalted butter
4 sliced small garlic cloves

8 thin slices of unpeeled lime
4 thin slices of unpeeled orange
4 6to 7ounce flounder or John Dory fillets (preferably with skin)
Cayenne pepper
8 fresh thyme sprigs, divided
8 tbsp. of dark beer
4 tbsp. of dry white wine
Corn and Tasso Maque Choux

Directions:
1. Cover the pan with a sheet of foil, leaving a long overhang on one facet. Separate the rings of one shallot and spread over the foil. Top with 1 tbsp. of butter, the sliced garlic clove, 2 lime slices, and an orange slice. Sprinkle one fillet on the two aspects with salt and Cayenne pepper. Put it, skin side down, on seasonings inside the pan. Top the filet with 2 thyme sprigs. Spoon 2 tbsp. of dark beer and 1 tbsp. wine across the fillet. Overlay lengthy foil overhang over the fillet to the inverse fringe of foil and bend the foil edge over to seal on three aspects. At that point, overlap once more to double seal. Move the parcel onto the baking sheet. Repeat with the final seasonings and fillets.
2. Set up the grill for high warmness. Place the parcels, constant facet up, at the grill. Cook till fish feels company whilst squeezed, round 10 mins. To be served with Corn and Tasso Maque Choux.

GRILLED ONION BUTTER COD

Ingredients:
1/4 cup butter
1 finely chopped small onion

1/4 cup white wine
4 (6ounce) cod fillets
1 tbsp. of extra virgin olive oil
1/2 tsp salt (or to taste) 1/2 tsp black
pepper lemon wedges

Directions:
1. Set up the grill for medium-high heat.
2. In a touch skillet liquefy the butter.
Add the onion and cook dinner for 1 or 2
minutes.
3. Add the white wine and let stew for an
additional 3 mins. Take away and let it cool
for 5 mins.
4. Spoon the fillets with greater virgin
olive oil and sprinkle with salt and pepper.
Put the fish on a well-oiled rack and cook
dinner for 8 minutes.
5. Season it with sauce and carefully turn
it over. Cook for 6 to 7 minutes more,
turning more instances or till the fish
arrives at an inner temperature of one
hundred forty-five F.
6. Take far away from the grill, top with
lemon wedges, and serve.

GRILLED BACON WRAPPED SCALLOPS WITH LEMON AIOLI

Ingredients:
2 tbsp. of red wine vinegar
2 tbsp. of olive oil
1 dash of black pepper
2 pounds' large fresh scallops
8 slices of bacon
For the Aioli:
1/2 cup mayonnaise
1 tbsp. lemon zest
1 tbsp. of fresh lemon juice
1 minced clove garlic

1 tsp Dijon mustard
1 dash of salt
1 tbsp. of flat-leaf parsley, finely
chopped

Directions:
1. Mix the vinegar, oil, and darkish pepper
in a medium bowl. Add the scallops to the
blend. Cover and permit it sit down for five
to 10 minutes at room temperature. Set
up the grill to medium-excessive heat. Cut
the bacon into thirds. Fold a bit of bacon
over every scallop and string onto skewers.
There should be 3 to four scallops for each
skewer.
2. Place the skewers on an oiled grate and
cook dinner for 3 to four minutes for every
side. When the scallops are darkened, take
away from the grill.
3. Prepare the lemon Aioli in a medium
bowl. Mix the mayonnaise with lemon
zest, lemon juice, the garlic, mustard, salt,
pepper, and parsley.
4. Spoon the bacon-wrapped scallops with
the lemon Aioli and serve.

TUNA CHOPS WITH LEMON CREAM SAUCE

Ingredients:
8 oz. tuna (2 fresh yellowfin steaks)
Kosher salt grounded black pepper
1 tsp of olive oil
2 tbsp. of butter
1/8 cup of sweet, minced onions
1 finely minced garlic clove
1/4 cup white wine
1 tsp of fresh lemon juice
1/4 cup cream (heavy)
2 tbsp. of capers, drained fresh dill weed
and lemon wedges

Directions:

1. Sprinkle both aspects of tuna steaks with Kosher salt and grounded pepper. Heat a heavy skillet over high warmness. Add the olive oil and one tbsp. of the butter and mix it all. Cook the tuna steaks until golden brown on each side, turning best once. Do not overcook tuna. Remove from the heat and keep heat.

2. Lower the heat to medium. Add the last butter and the onions. Gently sauté the onions. Add the garlic and sauté for another minute, stirring often. Slowly add in the white wine and the lemon juice and prepare dinner till the liquid is reduced to half, 2 or three mins. Add the cream, return to a simmer. Keep cooking for an extra three minutes or so until thickened. Add inside the capers. Spoon the lemon cream sauce over heat tuna steaks and garnish with dill and lemon or lime to serve.

GRILLED MUSHROOMS

Ingredients:
1/2-pound medium fresh mushrooms
1/4 cup of melted butter
1/2 tsp dill weed 1/2 tsp garlic salt
Directions:
1. String the mushrooms on four metallic or drenched wood skewers. Add the butter, dill, and garlic. Spoon the combination over the mushrooms and season with salt.
2. Grill the mushrooms over medium-high warmness for 1015 minutes, turning at everyday intervals.

PESTO CORN GRILLED PEPPERS

Ingredients:
1/2 cup plus 2 tsp of olive oil
3/4 cup of grated Parmesan
2 cups of packed basil leaves
2 tbsp. of sunflower kernels or walnuts
4 garlic cloves
1/2 cup of sweet red pepper
4 cups of thawed fresh or frozen corn
4 medium sweet red or yellow bell peppers
1/4 cup shredded Parmesan
Directions:
1. For the pesto, positioned half cup oil, floor Parmesan, basil, the sunflower kernels and garlic in a blender and blend it.
2. In a big skillet, put the ultimate oil and heat over medium-high warmth. Add the chopped red pepper and cook dinner until tender. Add the corn and pesto and preserve cooking for about one minute.
3. Cut the peppers in and expel the seeds. Grill the peppers over medium warmth, reduce side down, for approximately 8 mins. Turn and refill with corn mixture, then grill for 4 or 6 minutes longer. Serve with shredded Parmesan on top if you want it.

GRILLED CAULIFLOWER WEDGES

Ingredients:
1 large head of cauliflower
1 tsp ground turmeric
1/2 tsp of red pepper flakes 2 tbsp. of olive oil lemon juice olive oil pomegranate seeds, optional

Directions:

1. Take off the leaves and cut the cauliflower into eight wedges. Mix the turmeric and pepper flakes. Spoon the wedges with oil and sprinkle with turmeric mixture.

2. Grill over medium-excessive warmth approximately 810 minutes on each side. When served sprinkle with lemon juice and extra oil and present with pomegranate seeds, if you like it.

7

BASICS OF KAMADO

For a maximum of us, the kamado will now not be our first grill purchase. Many will come to the kamado after revel in with a protected kettle-fashion charcoal grill or a gasoline grill. Some techniques for the kamado will appear radically different from those cookers; however, there are several similarities. Some folks trust that it takes several years to become well versed in kamado cooking, and to that, I say, "hogwash!" Those who communicate with the venture of the kitchen in the kamado just don't need you to out cook them. There virtually may be a mastering curve, but that's to be anticipated. I assure you, inside more than one month, you'll be at the pinnacle of your kamado game. That said, you never actually forestall gaining knowledge of at the kamado; however, that's because the opportunities of what the grill can accomplish are so vast.

Cooking in Kamado

Despite my insistence that a kamado is the most flexible piece of outside cooking equipment, there are, in essence, basic setups for kamado cooking.

Direct Cooking

For grilling and searing. There's no barrier among the charcoal and the food. Cooking styles that use direct heat:+ì

- Grilling

160 - 180°C (320 - 360°F) - frequently cooking one aspect, flipping and cooking the other. You will but word that a kamado does still have an all-round prepare dinner effect on meals and isn't just one side or the alternative.

Searing

important sear marks too.

Other setups wherein you might use direct heat include:

- Wok Cooking

The wok stand is designed to direct the heat from your fireplace to the proper part of the wok. Cook with the bottom vent 1/2 open and lid open.

- Rotisserie

Bank the charcoal to one facet while using the rotisserie. Make fireplace out of 1/2 a dozen massive lumps of charcoal and add an extra one every now after which. Close the lid and hold the temperature among 150 - 180°C (300 - 350°F)

- Plancha or Fire Plate Cooking

Large fireplace plates are hot near the center and cooler to the outside. Great for communal cooking.

- Fish Plank

With the lowest vent closed, your kamado is like a fire pit. Cook with the lid open and a mild hearth.

- Kamado Tandoori

300°C (575°F) - Skewers, flatbreads, hot and fast cooking that seals inside the juices.

Indirect Cooking

The distinction between direct and indirect cooking in a kamado is the insertion of heat deflector stones between the charcoal heat supply and the meals, thus remodeling the kamado from a grill to a conference oven.

Note: Half-moon deflector stones coupled with a charcoal basket divider with segregate your kamado, providing 50% direct heat and 50% convection warmth. Use the indirect set up for:

Smoking

110 -125°C (225 - 260°F). Add timber chunks on your charcoal fireplace and cook dinner meats at these low temperatures for long durations of time

Roasting 180 - 220°C (350 - 430°F). Ideal for large gentle meat joints, beer can bird, and your Christmas turkey. Any traditional oven recipe is ideal for kamado cooking, although it could cook a little faster and be organized for high-quality consequences.

Baking

140 - 200°C (285 - 390°F) Use the pizza stone over the warmth deflector stones for pastries and pieces of bread. Depending on how you prepare dinner, you might also need to start with a chilly pizza stone.

Braising or Dutch Oven Cooking

135 - 165°C (275 - 325°F). Leave a fantastic air hole between the heat deflector stones and the grill grate upon which your vicinity you pan.

Pizza

325 - 350°C (620 - 700°F). A ceramic kamado is ideal for cooking at those high temperatures and delivers excellent pizza in just minutes. A correct air gap between the heat deflector stones and the pizza stone is the high-quality installation and gives your pizza stone lots of time to stand up to temperature.

Plank Cooking

110 - 180°C (230 - 350°C). Fish cooked low at the lower stop of the temperature scale with a few timber chips on the coals for brought flavor. But then this hen stuffed with garlic, cheese, and wrapped in bacon become notable too!

Clean Down

To clean the outdoors of a kamado, cart and facet tables, use water and mild cleaning agent. Never use water to smooth the inside of a kamado.

The interior may be cleaned through the use of high temperatures. Remove all stainless steel components before commencing. Completely open both top and backside vents (make sure there's enough charcoal inside the firebox).

Raise the temperature to 400°C and go away for 10 minutes. Be careful not to exceed 400 °C due to the fact this will harm the gasket.

After the kamado has cooled down, put off any ash from the ceramic additives with a soft brush and easy the grill grates with a wire brush.

Smoking in Kamado

I cooked the maximum tremendous barbeque you've ever eaten on a kamado, and you simply needed to have one. Congratulations, you are now the proprietor of a lean, mean backyard smoking machine!

Whether you are smoking a soft reduce like pork tenderloin, intending to be prepared to experience in just an hour, or harder cuts like brisket or red meat shoulder, to stay inside the kamado for many, many hours before falling into delicious strands on the prod of a fork, you're embarking on a culinary journey with a reliable guide at your aspect, the kamado.

I've smoked on pretty much every possible grill to be had to the home pit master—side-container smokers, bullet smokers, kettles, even oil drum rigs. Nothing has outperformed the kamado. Smoking temperatures typically range from 150° F ("cold smoking" and perfect for fish) to 225° F, with the outside variety being 275° F. Times for smoking can run as short as an hour, or 8 hours or extra. It takes precision with temperature to smoke correctly. If smoking isn't your daily activity, the kamado is your precision tool.

The insulating homes of the ceramic-clad kamado, coupled with its damper gadget and elliptical or oval design, are a match made in smoking heaven. With the kamado, temperature management is nearly as easy as flipping a switch after you grow to be familiar, along with your unique grill. Of the five distinctive racks from five specific manufacturers that I have cooked with at the same time as penning this book, I have been capable of maintaining 200° F in all, however, one for sixteen hours without adding any more charcoal. Imagine loading your kamado with charcoal and understanding that probabilities are you will no longer mess with your fireplace again!

Also, maximum meals will cook dinner or smoke quicker inside the kamado because of its tight seal and superior insulation. While there's no want to boost the lid to restore the hearth, the heat retention is even higher.

Smoking can frequently motive foods to dry out. That's why, when smoking, you're regularly instructed to position a water pan inside the grill. But not within the kamado. The tight seal keeps water from evaporating, and alternatively, it condenses at the pinnacle of the dome. A few years ago on the Big Apple Barbecue Block Party in New York City, I asked pitmaster Mike Mills, a past Memphis in May Champion and Bill Clinton's cross-to guy for ribs (Mike had a clearance on Air

Force One to supply ribs), why there was so little smoke coming from his rig.

The setup for smoking inside the kamado differs barely for each brand (make sure to examine your manual), however basically, it's the same. A fire is built, then a ceramic plate (consider it as flame tamer) is set over the light on the lower rack, below the grate where the meals will sit. This setup blocks the food from the direct warmness of the fire. It is also possible putting a solid iron skillet or grill pan on that decrease rack. I've had the right achievement doing this.

When on the point of smoke, I even have found that going for walks the temperature beyond the target smoking temperature, say 300° F while I need to smoke at 225° F, is helpful. By the time I've opened the dome, inserted the ceramic plate, and positioned my food at the grill, my temperature has generally dropped to my goal temperature, and I'm ready to cook. I then regulate the dampers to maintain that temperature. With almost every model of kamado that I tested, I attempt to have the top damper open only slightly, and the lowest open approximately an inch or two.

Your meals will grow to be with a pleasant smoky taste if you just use lump charcoal and not anything else, but you can add wood chunks to amp up the smokiness or add another taste profile. For each recipe in this chapter (except for a handful of methods where I think additional smoke doesn't work with the flavors involved), I come up with my advice of what timber will work pleasant; you may additionally omit the wooden entirely. You can soak the chunks or no longer, it's as much as you. I locate it unnecessary—sections that smoke from the get-cross, and as they burn, they become the own charcoal. Also, don't stress too much approximately having the chunks smoking via the entire cooking time. Most proteins take at the lion's share in their smoke taste within the first hours of smoking.

Grilling in Kamado

Grilling, through definition, is cooking over direct heat, and it's no exceptional on a kamado. Direct grilling is speedy and warm, with complete publicity of the meals to the charcoal fireplace. The result is beautifully seared and caramelized surfaces and a juicy interior.

Yes, you need a warm hearth to grill. No, it doesn't need to be 700° F. Great grilling may be accomplished anywhere from 400° to 700° F. I've located that 500° F works properly for maximum all meals and is an excellent starting point. Some items, like beef and fowl, decide on a lower temperature, around 400° F, any better and that they'll in all likelihood toughen. Please follow the goal temperatures I come up with in every recipe.

Not every kind of food is reducing out for direct heat. Pick foods that are soft and generally no more than inches thick, and that might cook dinner inside 20 mins or less in any cooking circumstance. Steaks, chops, burgers, hen parts, fish (each fillet or steaks and entire small fish), whole short cuts like pork tenderloin, and vegetables enter into this category.

When grilling in a kamado, the dome needs to be closed. Remember the kamado mantra: "If it isn't closed, it isn't cooking." Everything approximately the advanced effects that come from a kamado is about retaining the dome closed, so when you do open it (to show or baste your meals or positioned cheese on burgers), work quickly.

For grilling, you need a hot hearth, and there are numerous matters to preserve in thoughts in that regard. First, best use lump charcoal; it burns hotter, longer, and, maximum importantly, is ready to cook dinner on faster than briquettes. With lump charcoal, you're correct to cross simply as soon as you notice a touch gray.

Don't be bashful approximately the amount of charcoal you use; any unused charcoal will relight the following time you operate the kamado. Start with large pieces on the bottom, with the portions getting regularly smaller as you build the pile. Have the upper and lower dampers open all of the way open, and inside five to 10 mins of lighting your hearth, insert the grill grate and near the dome. Then let the kamado take over; when you hit your target temperature, regulate the dampers to hold it. If you locate your fireplace has gotten a bit out of manage, the quickest way to adjust the temperature down is to cautiously open the dome for a moment, modify the dampers, and then close the dome.

You may not have offered the kamado with grilling in mind; however, my kamado has outperformed each grill I very own, each gas and charcoal, in this project of direct warmness. The meals always have a pleasant, more nuance of smoke remains moister, and has a proper char. It virtually is the go-to grill for all forms of out of doors cooking.

Roasting in Kamado

Roasting on a kamado grill is even better than using your indoor oven.

Your oven can't provide you with that extra layer of woodsy

taste that you get from cooking outdoors, or the wet cooking environment the kamado grill is built to deliver. When you roast within the kamado, meals will cook dinner quicker, with more even browning, and grow to be moister and delicious than in case you cooked it on your oven.

Roasting takes location everywhere from 350° to 500°F. You might be cooking indirectly; in different words, the warmth will now not make direct contact with the meals.

The key to success is the barrier among the fire and the meals. You can set up your kamado simply as you'll for smoking, the use of a ceramic plate as that barrier, or you could place your meals in a roasting pan (you may even use a disposable aluminum-foil pan), cast-iron skillet, or baking sheet. The benefit of roasting in a container is that you'll turn out to be with the makings for nice pan gravy.

In a number of the recipes in this chapter, you'll see that I begin with starting my meals immediately over the hearth to get some tasty browning and caramelization, then circulate to indirect cooking and lower grill temperature. You'll find the precise temperatures indicated in every recipe. And losing from a higher temperature to a decrease temperature isn't challenging to do. Let's say you're searing a beef tenderloin. When you open the dome to set it on the grill, the temperature starts losing. By the time you're done searing and feature inserted the ceramic plate or positioned the tenderloin in a roasting pan and returned it to the grill, the temperature may additionally have dropped 100 degrees, getting you for your roasting temperature. Now all you need to do is near the dome and modify the dampers to keep this decreasing temperature. I strongly inspire you to invest in a probe thermometer that allows you to assist you in monitoring the internal temperature of your meals without starting the dome. Remember the kamado mantra: "If it isn't closed, it isn't cooking." This following is an exciting chapter with some admittedly over-the-top flavors. Try them all, to the satisfaction of your circle of relatives and friends. While a lot of us consider the kamado as a smoker, I'm here to inform you it's additionally a roasting machine!

Steaming and Braising in Kamado

I expected my kamado to be a first-rate smoker. And it had to be a first-rate grill. Roasting, sure, it should be able to cope with that with ease. But my biggest marvel has been what an unusual activity of steaming and braising the kamado grill does. The kamado indeed can do it all with little paintings or worry on our part.

With steaming, food is cooked, commonly in a blanketed pot on the stovetop, over a small amount of boiling water. Food that is steamed tends to hold more of its nutrients and herbal texture and flavor, a boon for higher raw foods.

Braising, on the other hand, requires that the beef or vegetable be browned first and then cooked in liquid at low heat, included, for a reasonably long time. This technique breaks down tough fibers, tenderizing the meals, and excessive flavors develop. Braising is a giant buddy to tougher cuts of meat like lamb shanks and lean pork roasts, and arrangements like a stew.

So why do I like to use the kamado for steaming and braising? Because it does each so properly. Its precise temperature to manipulate and creates an environment in which you may "set it and overlook it"—your very own grilling gradual cooker, as it were. You can get the added gain of the smoke flavor, in the case of steamed dishes, like Old-Fashioned Oyster Roast. They are cooked properly at the grill or, in braising, the dishes wherein the beef is first browned off on the grill directly over the fire, and then transferred to its braising liquid and finished off inside the kamado.

The grill set up is accessible for each steaming and braising— crank up the roast just as you will for direct warmness and use the dampers to govern the temperatures. Most of the temperatures might be inside the midrange, among 300° and 400° F. Don't get panicked if the temperature ranges off no longer precisely where I've indicated. In most of the braising recipes, I'll have you ever begin at a higher temperature to brown the protein, after which drop the temperature to braise. The kamado facilitates you with this, the temperature inside the grill losing barely on every occasion you open the dome to show the protein while browning it.

While you don't want ceramic plates or different kamado grill equipment for steaming and braising, you do need some heavy-responsibility pots and baking dishes. I like forged iron and porcelain-coated forged iron. You'll additionally want a roll of heavy-obligation aluminum foil as well as disposable aluminum-foil roasting pans and pie plates. Add a steaming rack to your arsenal, and you could steam large quantities of shrimp, mollusks, or corn, for instance. With your kamado added to the temperature at 350° F, it needs to take less than 10 minutes for the steam to build within the pot; add your meals, cowl the container, close the dome, and steam till performed. Five pounds of shrimp will generally take no longer than 15 minutes.

By this point on this cookbook, you would possibly think I've gone past the point of obsession with my kamado. But no, I consider in putting my cooking device thru its paces, to see what the bounds of its makes use of are, even past what it's miles marketed to do. And what I've observed is that the kamado steams and braises as well as it smokes. Just name it getting your money's well worth from an outstanding investment!

Baking inside the Kamado

My grandmother had approaches to cook dinner in her rural North Carolina home —one of those newfangled (to her) electric-powered stoves and her trusty wooden stove. It took her a while to trust the electric stove, and most mornings, her biscuits came from the wood-fired oven—and they were the satisfactory biscuits I have ever eaten. That timber oven brought something specific to her cookies that electric or gasoline just couldn't deliver— an essence of smoke and an outer crispness that belied their soft, flaky insides. I concept that turned into lost forever until I purchased a kamado grill and realized what an exquisite baking apparatus it's far.

Wood-fired ovens are all of the rages in the restaurant and bakery international, and with good reason—the tasty outcomes yielded from cooking with timber communicate for themselves. And the kamado's excellent heat retention and precise temperature manipulate, at the side of its ability to lure moisture and flow into warmth perfectly, mimics and improves upon the wooden- or charcoal-fired brick oven.

I used to be what is known in the culinary world as a "bone roaster." Give me meat to cook dinner, and I turned into happy.

That changed while I was given my kamado. Now I like to bake pieces of bread, pies, and cakes inside the kamado, and I've had a blast with breakfast gadgets in addition to baked entrees. The kamado has made it smooth like a laugh to bake high-quality crusty bread. Also, experiencing naan proper off cooked on the grill, that supply a further taste to the fish. Moreover, baking a pie that receives a double dose of apple flavor since I can cook dinner it over an Applewood hearth, or delight with a pizza excellent than as y you could buy at a wood-fired oven pizzeria.

So how does it happen? The baking occurs from 300° F to 450°-500° F, however mostly inside the decrease range. This way is what differentiates it from roasting, wherein you use higher temperatures to help create a tasty crust on your meals.

Baking is an indirect method of cooking, which means the meals will now not come immediately in contact with the flame. In the recipes that follow, you'll see that that is executed in several methods. In the first and most effective technique, the dish is placed at the grill grate in a cooking vessel. Cast-iron is a top-notch desire for this; however, anything this is flameproof will work.

Second, the ceramic plate is inserted within the kamado and allowed to heat up thoroughly. The food is either positioned immediately on that plate or in a cooking vessel at the plate. In this case, you don't should use flameproof cookware; ovenproof—like Pyrex—will work fine.

The ceramic plate is inserted, and a baking stone or pizza stone is positioned on top of that. The baking is allowed to heat up earlier than the meals are placed without the delay of heating. I think about this "stone on stone" cooking. It's crucial to cook pizza the use of this technique, as the stone attracts moisture from the crust because it bakes, supplying you with that authentic, crispy crust which you can't gain in an indoor oven or, for that matter, some other grill I've ever tried. Once you've made pizza to your kamado, I doubt you'll ever choose up the phone again to call for delivery. Suppose you need to select the method that's the least problem for you. There's undoubtedly no right or wrong manner.

If you'd like to provide your meals a further shot of smoke even as it's cooking, you could add wood chunks (now not chips). Don't trouble to soak them in advance. Just be sure to pick wood to play quality together with your meals, like cherry wooden for a berry crisp. Hickory is a little sturdy for maximum baking, however maybe tasty when firing up a pizza.

Temperature management is essential while baking in your Kamado, and you need to withstand the temptation to open the dome. That said, don't panic over mild temperature variations even as your dish is baking. That occurs in your indoor oven as nicely, and it's simply not made evident to you as it's far with the temperature gauge on the front of your kamado. It takes a little exercise to bake in a kamado; however, I doubt which you'll destroy any meals along the way.

There are exceptional recipes in this chapter, and I desire you try them all. When it comes to baking, the kamado all over again verified its well worth as a multitasking cooking marvel.

KAMADO RECIPES

Kamado Grill recipes are not only for personal enjoyment but also for family enjoyment.

You will love them for sure for how easy it is to prepare them.

SIMPLE KAMADO CHICKEN

Preparation Time: 30 minutes
Cooking Time: 4 hours
Servings: 4-6

Ingredients:
1 chicken
Brine
3 L water
1 cup of salt
1 cup of sugar
Maple Glaze
1 cup maple syrup
2 tablespoons butter
1 tsp thyme
1 tsp garlic powder
Directions:
1. In a pan add water, salt, and sugar
2. Add the hen and refrigerate for 1-2 hours
3. In a bowl combine all components for the brine
4. Brush the bird with the mixture
5. When ready vicinity the fowl in the grill
6. Brush again with the last glaze
7. Cook for 3-four hours until it receives to a hundred 65 F
8. When ready cast off from the barbeque and serve.

LEMON CHICKEN

Preparation Time: 10 minutes
Cooking Time: 60 minutes
Servings: 4-6

Ingredients:
1 chicken
2 lemons
½ cup of salt
½ cup pepper
Directions:
1. Sprinkle the chicken with salt and pepper
2. Squeeze the juice from one lemon over the chook and rub
3. Refrigerate for 1-2 hours
4. four. Preheat the grill at three hundred F
5. Place the bird on the rack and prepare

dinner for 60 mins

6. Turn the bird every 15 minutes and squeeze lemon juice over

7. When ready do away with from the grill and serve.

SIMPLE KAMADO CHICKEN

Preparation Time: 10 minutes
Cooking Time: 60 hours
Servings: 4-6

Ingredients:
1 chicken
½ cup of salt
½ cup pepper
2-3 cloves garlic

Directions:
1. Cut the chook and sprinkle with salt and pepper
2. Place the garlic gloves inside
3. Refrigerate for 1-2 hours
4. Grill at three hundred F for 60 mins
5. When ready do away with from the rack and serve.

SOUTHWESTERN BBQ CHICKEN

Preparation Time: 1 hours
Cooking Time: 2 hours
Servings: 4-6

Ingredients:
2 tsp chili powder
1 tsp garlic powder
1 tsp cumin powder
1 tsp onion powder
1 tsp smoked paprika

1 tsp salt
1 chicken

Directions:
1. Mix all species
2. Cut the fowl into pieces
3. Rub the fowl with the mixture
4. Grill the hen pieces at three hundred F
5. Turn every 15 mins
6. When ready get rid of from the oven and serve.

PORK

APPLE CIDER GLAZED PORK CHOPS

Ingredients:
3 pounds' pork chops
Rub
1 1/2 tablespoons kosher salt
1 tablespoon garlic powder
2 teaspoons ground black pepper
Glaze
1 cup apple cider
1 tablespoon apple cider vinegar
2 tablespoons honey
2 tablespoons 100% pure maple syrup
1 tablespoon Dijon mustard

Directions:
1. In a small blending bowl, whisk collectively rub ingredients. Generously rub the mixture on both sides of beef and set aside.
2. Heat glaze elements in a small saucepan over medium-high warmness. Turn warmness right down to low as soon as it begins to simmer and permit simmer for five mins. Remove from

warmth and let cool.

3. Preheat grill to 500°F. Grill red meat chops over direct warmth for approximately 12 mins, flipping every 2 mins (about 6 minutes total in keeping with a side). Glaze the beef chops the remaining couple instances you flip. Once the internal temperature of the red meat reaches one hundred 45°F, put off from grill and let rest five-10 mins.

SPICY DRY RUBBED PULLED PORK TACOS

Ingredients:
8 pounds' pork shoulder
taco shells
cilantro, for garnish
lime
wood chips, if desired Taco Dry Rub
1 tablespoon chili powder
1 tablespoon cumin
1 tablespoon ancho chipotle powder
1 tablespoon garlic powder
1 tablespoon kosher salt
1 tablespoon black pepper
1 teaspoon onion powder
1 teaspoon Mexican oregano
1 teaspoon crushed red pepper
1 teaspoon cayenne pepper
Directions:
1. In a medium mixing bowl, whisk together taco seasoning rub. Rub all of it over pork shoulder.
2. Preheat grill to 250F and load with masses of sparkling charcoal.
3. Place red meat shoulder on the roasting rack and place it on the grill. Add wood chips if using them (maintain to add every hour if you need a robust flavor).

4. Grill on oblique warmth for 16 hours or till the internal temperature of the beef reaches 195F. Remove from grill and permit rest for 15-30 minutes. Cut and put on tortilla shells with cilantro and lime.

Notes
5. Plan on smoking the beef shoulder for about 2 hours consistent with a pound of meat plus an additional 1-2-hour cushion.
6. There is usually a stall zone around one hundred 65-180F.

WRAPPED TENDERLOINS

Serves: 4
Prep Time: 10Minutes
Cook Time: 60Minutes
Total Time: 70Minutes

Ingredients:
2 lb. pork tenderloins
1 cup mustard
1 tablespoon peppercorn
6 sage leaves
6-8 slices bacon
8-10 bamboo skewers
Directions:
1. Cut the tenderloin and spread mustard in a thick layer over the beef
2. Scatter peppercorns evenly
3. Sprinkle sage leaves and deform bacon slices around the tenderloin
4. Grill at four hundred F till the indoors hits a hundred 45 F
5. When ready put off from heat and serve

Serves: 4-6
Prep Time: 10 Minutes
Cook Time: 4 Hours
Total Time: 4 Hours 10 Minutes 6

Ingredients:
2 lb. pork loin ribs
2 tablespoons salt
¼ tsp celery seeds
1 tablespoon paprika
1 tsp sage
1 cup apple juice
Directions:
1. In a bowl integrate all substances, except pork loin ribs, and blend well.
2. Place the beef in the mixture and let it marinate for 2-3 hours.
3. Place the ribs at the grill.
4. Cook for 3-four hours and brush with apple juice while turning the red meat.
5. Serve while ready.

Serves: 4-6
Prep Time: 10 Minutes
Cook Time: 4 Hours
Total Time: 4 Hours 10 Minutes

Ingredients:
4-6 spare ribs
1 cup mustard
1 cup BBQ sauce
Directions:
1. Coat the ribs with mustard and BBQ sauce
2. Let them marinate overnight.
3. Grill at 400 F for three-4 hours.

4. When ready do away with from the grill and serve.

Serves: 4
Prep Time: 10 Minutes
Cook Time: 2 Hours
Total 2 Hours 10 Minutes

Ingredients:
1 pork loin filet
1/4 cup granulated garlic
1 tsp salt
2 cups mushroom stuffing
Directions:
1. Poke a hole in the pork loin fillet
2. Spoon the mushroom filling into the hole.
3. Season the outdoor of the red meat loin fillet with granulated garlic and salt.
4. Roast for 12-15 minutes at 275 F
5. Cook till the roast is a hundred 65 F around 1- 1.30h.
6. When ready take away and serve.

BEEF

Serves: 6-8
Prep Time: 10 Minutes
Cook Time: 30 Minutes
Total Time: 40 Minutes

Ingredients:
2 lbs. ground beef

2 tablespoons garlic powder
1 tsp salt
1 tsp black pepper
Directions:
1. In a bowl integrate all ingredients collectively and blend well.
2. Shape meat into hamburger patties
3. Grill at 400 F for 5-10 minutes in step with side.
4. When ready get rid of from the oven and serve.

ARROWHEAD BURGERS

Serves: 6-8
Prep Time: 10 Minutes
Cook Time: 30 Minutes
Total Time: 40 Minutes

Ingredients:
3 lb. ground beef
1 tsp sage
1 tsp garlic powder
1 tsp thyme
1 tsp salt
1 tsp pepper
Directions:
1. In a bowl integrate all ingredients and mix well.
2. Shape meat into hamburger patties
3. Grill at four hundred F for 5-10 minutes in line with the side.
4. When ready eliminate from the oven and serve.

GRILLED STEAK FAJITAS

Serves: 4
Prep Time: 10 Minutes
Cook Time: 30 Minutes

Total Time: 40 Minutes

Ingredients:
2 lb. sirloin strip steak
½ cup olive oil
juice one lime
1 tsp garlic powder
1 tablespoon onion powder
¼ tsp nutmeg
1 tsp salt
Directions:
1. In a bowl integrate all ingredients collectively and blend well.
2. Place meat in a marinade and let the beef marinate overnight.
3. Preheat the grill at 450 F.
4. Grill steak approximately 5-6 minutes in line with the side until the temperature reaches a hundred and fifty-five F
5. When ready take away from heat and serve.

CHEESE BURGERS

Serves: 6
Prep Time: 10 Minutes
Cook Time: 30 Minutes
Total Time: 40 Minutes

Ingredients:
2 lbs. ground beef
½ cup BBQ sauce
1 tablespoon pepper sauce
1 bunch scallion
1 tsp garlic powder
1 tsp black pepper
1 cup blue cheese crumbles
Directions:
1. In a bowl combine all ingredients and blend well.

2. Shape meat into hamburger patties.
3. Grill at 400 F for 5-10 minutes in line with the side.
4. When ready take away from the oven and serve.

HOMEMADE BURGERS

Serves: 6
Prep Time: 10 Minutes
Cook Time: 30 Minutes
Total Time: 40 Minutes

Ingredients:
2 tsp paprika
2 lb. ground beef
2 tsp black pepper
2 tsp salt
2 tsp brown sugar
2 tsp garlic powder
2 tsp onion powder
Directions:
1. In a bowl integrate all ingredients collectively and mix well.
2. Shape meat into hamburger patties
3. Grill at 400 F for 5-10 minutes according to side.
4. When ready put off from the oven and serve.

POT ROAST

Serves: 6
Prep Time: 10 Minutes
Cook Time: 60 Minutes
Total Time: 70 Minutes

Ingredients:
pot roast
¼ tsp salt

¼ tsp black pepper
1 cup seasoning
Directions:
1. Season the roast with salt, pepper, and seasoning.
2. Preheat the grill to 400 F.
3. Grill the roast until it reaches a hundred 65 F.
4. When ready get rid of from warmness and serve.

GRILLED BRISKET

Serves: 4-6
Prep Time: 10 Minutes
Cook Time:60 Minutes
Total Time: 70 Minutes

Ingredients:
6 lb. brisket
Dry Rub
1 tablespoon salt
1 tablespoon chili powder
1 tablespoon brown sugar
1 tsp cumin
1 tsp black pepper
1 tsp paprika
1 tsp onion powder
Directions:
1. Season the roast with salt, pepper, and seasoning.
2. Preheat the grill to 400 F
3. Grill the roast till it reaches a hundred 65 F.
4. When ready take away from heat and serve.

KAMADO GRILL BACON BRUSSEL SPROUTS

Serves: 4
Prep Time: 10Minutes
Cook Time: 30Minutes
Total Time: 40Minutes

Ingredients:
1 lb. bacon
20-30 Brussels sprouts
Directions:
1. Cut bacon in 1/2 and wrap the bacon around the Brussels sprouts
2. Preheat the grill to 225 F
3. Cook for 30-35 minutes
4. When ready put off from heat and serve.

MARINATE, RUBS, AND SAUCES

BUFFALO SAUCE

Serves: 1
Prep Time: 5 Minutes
Cook Time: 5 Minutes
Total Time: 10 Minutes

Ingredients:
1 cup hot pepper sauce
¼ cup tomato sauce
1 tsp apple cider vinegar
1 tsp garlic powder
1 tsp black pepper
Directions:
1. In a bowl combine all components.
2. Mix nicely and use for marinade.

CHIMICHURRI SAUCE

Serves: 1
Prep Time: 5 Minutes
Cook Time: 5 Minutes
Total Time: 10Minutes

Ingredients:
1 cup cilantro
2 crushed cloves garlic
2 cups parsley
¼ cup olive oil
2 tsp red pepper flakes
1 tsp paprika
¼ tsp salt
Directions:
1. Place all ingredients in a blender and blend until smooth.
2. Place in a bowl and use for marinade.

TACO SEASONING

Serves: 1
Prep Time: 5 Minutes
Cook Time:5 Minutes
Total Time: 10Minutes

Ingredients:
1 tablespoon chili powder
1 tablespoon cumin
1 tablespoon garlic powder
1 tablespoon salt
1 tablespoon black pepper
1 tablespoon onion powder
1 tsp Mexican spices
1 tsp smoked paprika
Directions:
1. Place all substances in a blender and blend till clean.
2. Place in a bowl and use for marinade.

LEBANESE SAUCE

Serves: 1
Prep Time: 5 Minutes
Cook Time: 5 Minutes
Total Time: 10 Minutes

Ingredients:
1 cup cloves garlic
1 tsp salt
½ cup lemon juice
1 cup olive oil
Directions:
1. Place all ingredients in a blender and blend until clean.
2. Place in a bowl and use for marinade.

TAMARIND DIPPING SAUCE

Serves: 1
Prep Time: 5 Minutes
Cook Time: 5 Minutes
Total Time: 10 Minutes

Ingredients:
1 cup peanuts
1 tablespoon brown sugar
2 cloves garlic
2 tablespoon soy sauce
2 tablespoons curry paste
1 tablespoon tamarind concentrate
1 tablespoon olive oil
Directions:
1. Place all substances in a blender and blend till smooth.
2. Place in a bowl and use for marinade.

AIOLI SAUCE

Serves: 1
Prep Time: 5 Minutes
Cook Time: 5 Minutes
Total Time: 10 Minutes

Ingredients:
1 egg
2 cloves garlic
2 tsp lemon juice
½ cup olive oil
¼ tsp salt
Directions:
1. Place all components in a blender and blend till easy.
2. Place in a bowl and use for marinade.

YEMENITE SAUCE

Serves: 1
Prep Time: 5 Minutes
Cook Time: 5 Minutes
Total Time: 10 Minutes

Ingredients:
½ tsp coriander seed
½ tsp cumin seeds
½ tsp black pepper
2 cardamom pods
2 cloves garlic
1 tsp salt
2 oz. parsley
¼ cup olive oil
Directions:
1. Place all ingredients in a blender and blend until clean.
2. Place in a bowl and use for marinad.

MINT MOJO

Serves: 1
Prep Time: 5 Minutes
Cook Time: 5 Minutes
Total Time: 10 Minutes

Ingredients:
¼ cup mint leaves
1 cup parsley
1 clove garlic
1 tablespoon lemon zest
1 shallot
1 smoked paprika
1 tsp
Directions:
1. Place all elements in a blender and blend until easy.
2. Place in a bowl and use for marinade.

GARDEN PESTO

Serves: 1
Prep Time: 5 Minutes
Cook Time: 5 Minutes
Total Time: 10 Minutes

Ingredients:
1 cup cilantro leaves
1 cup basil leaves
½ cup parsley leaves
½ cup pistachios
2 cloves garlic
1 tsp miso
¼ cup olive oil
Directions:
1. Place all elements in a blender and blend till smooth.
2. Place in a bowl and use for marinade.

ROASTED-FENNEL PESTO

Serves: 1
Prep Time: 5 Minutes
Cook Time: 5 Minutes
Total Time: 10 Minutes

Ingredients:
1 cup fennel bulb
1 cup olive oil
¼ cup almonds
½ cup fennel fronds
2 cloves garlic
1 tsp salt
Directions:
1. Place all ingredients in a blender and blend until smooth.
2. Place in a bowl and use for marinade.

HONEY DIPPING SAUCE

Serves: 1
Prep Time: 5 Minutes
Cook Time: 5 Minutes
Total Time: 10 Minutes

Ingredients:
4 tablespoons melted butter
6 tablespoons kimchi paste
1 tablespoon honey
1 tsp sesame seeds
Directions:
1. Place all elements in a blender and blend till clean.
2. Place in a bowl and use for marinade.

GINGER DIPPING SAUCE

Serves: 1
Prep Time: 5 Minutes
Cook Time: 5 Minutes
Total Time: 10 Minutes

Ingredients:
6 tablespoons ponzu sauce
2 tablespoons scallions
2 tsp ginger
2 tsp mirin
2 tsp sesame oil
¼ tsp salt
Directions:
1. Place all substances in a blender and blend until clean.
2. Place in a bowl and use for marinade.

THAI SAUCE

Serves: 1
Prep Time: 5 Minutes
Cook Time:5 Minutes
Total Time: 10 Minutes

Ingredients:
6 oz. garlic
2 tablespoons Asian sauce
2 tablespoons lime juice
2 tablespoons brown sugar
2 tablespoons cilantro leaves
1 tsp chili flakes
Directions:
1. Place all ingredients in a blender and blend till easy.
2. Place in a bowl and use for marinade.

TANGY BBQ SAUCE

Serves: 1
Prep Time: 5 Minutes
Cook Time: 5 Minutes
Total Time: 10 Minutes

Ingredients:
1 tablespoon olive oil
¼ red onion
1 tablespoon tomato paste
¼ tsp cumin
1 can tomato puree
1 tablespoon cider vinegar
1 tsp mustard
1 tsp salt
1 tsp liquid smoke
Directions:
1. Place all elements in a blender and blend till clean.
2. Place in a bowl and use for marinade.

POMEGRANATE BARBEQUE SAUCE

Serves: 1
Prep Time: 5 Minutes
Cook Time: 5 Minutes
Total Time: 10 Minutes

Ingredients:
2 tablespoons olive oil
¼ cup red onion
¼ tsp salt
¼ tsp black pepper
1 clove garlic
1 cup tomato sauce
¼ cup red wine vinegar
¼ cup pomegranate molasses
2 tablespoons lime juice

2 tablespoons tamari sauce
Directions:
1. Place all ingredients in a blender and blend till clean.
2. Place in a bowl and use for marinade.

ROASTED TOMATILLO SAUCE

Serves: 1
Prep Time: 5 Minutes
Cook Time: 5 Minutes
Total Time: 10Minutes

Ingredients:
6 oz. tomatillos
½ cup black pepper
2 cloves garlic
2 tablespoons olive oil
¼ tsp salt
Directions:
1. Place all substances in a blender and blend until smooth.
2. Place in a bowl and use for marinade.

SMOKED KAMADO

SMOKED GARLIC BEEF TENDERLOIN

Beef tenderloin is always a treat. Add smoke and low and slow cooking, and the result is a butter knife-tender piece of beef infused with the essence of wood. This method adds so much flavor to the tenderloin, actually enhancing its beefiness. It's a perfect choice for large gatherings and deliciously warm, at room temperature, or even cold (it makes a killer roast beef sandwich). For a flavor change-up, swap out the regular garlic for smoke-roasted garlic.

Serves 8 to 12
Ingredients:
10 cloves garlic
1 teaspoon kosher salt
1 tablespoon chopped fresh thyme
1 tablespoon chopped fresh flat-leaf parsley
1 (4-pound) beef tenderloin roast, trimmed of silver skin
Freshly ground black pepper
Prepared horseradish sauce
<u>Recommended wood: Hickory</u>
Directions:
1. Using the butt of the knife, smash every garlic clove on a slicing board and peel it. Sprinkle the cloves with the salt and mash the garlic to obtain a paste, working with the knife back and forth. Place the garlic paste in a small bowl and paintings in the herbs. Smear the paste all over the beef, ensuring you get the ends as well. Liberally season with black pepper. Place the tenderloin on a cord rack and then place the grill in a disposable aluminum-foil pan to trap the drippings.
2. Light a fireplace in the kamado grill using your favorite method. After approximately 10 minutes, close the dome and open the higher and lower dampers all the way. When the temperature reaches 300° F, location the wooden chunks around the fire and uploads any add-ons essential for smoking on your precise grill, in conjunction with the grill rack. Close the dome, let the temperature build back to

between 200° and 250° F, and watch for a bit.

3. Place the pan at the grill, near the dome, and smoke the roast for approximately 2 hours. Cook the meat until the inner temperature inside the middle reaches 125° F for rare or in your desired diploma of doneness.

4. Transfer the roast to a slicing board and allow rest for an approximate half-hour, tented with foil, if preferred. Slice the roast thinly and serve with horseradish sauce at the facet and any accumulated pan drippings.

KANSAS CITY PRIME RIB

Do you remember back in the '80s when every restaurant had the ubiquitous prime rib night? It may have fallen out of favor with restaurant diners, but savvy cooks know better. Taking the time to smoke a prime rib adds that final nuance of delicious flavor to this exquisite cut of meat, elevating it to truly regal status.

Serves: 8 to 10
Ingredients:
5 bone-in standing rib roast (about 6 pounds), trimmed of excess fat
6 large cloves garlic, peeled
2 tablespoons fresh rosemary leaves
2 tablespoons fresh thyme leaves
Kosher salt and freshly ground black pepper
2 tablespoons coarse-grain Dijon mustard
3 tablespoons olive oil
Prepared horseradish sauce
Recommended wood: Hickory

Directions:
1. At least 1 hour earlier than you're ready to begin cooking, cast off the roast from the refrigerator. In a food processor or mortar, integrate the garlic, rosemary, thyme, and 2 teaspoons each salt and pepper. Pulse to mince or weigh down with a pestle finely. Add the mustard and pulse or blend to integrate. Slowly add the oil with the food processor running or gradually blend in with the pestle until paste forms. Smear the paste flippantly over the whole floor of the roast. For a more excessive herb taste, let the roast sit down at room temperature for two hours or wrap and refrigerate overnight.

2. Light a fire within the kamado grill the use of your preferred method. After about 10 minutes, near the dome and open the higher and decrease dampers all of the ways. When the temperature reaches 300° F, place the wooden chunks around the fire and add any add-ons essential for smoking on your unique grill, alongside the grill rack. Close the dome, permit the temperature to build lower back to among 200° and 250° F, and watch for a bit smoke to accumulate. Adjust the dampers to preserve the heat on this range.

3. Place the roast, bone aspect down, on a rack in a disposable aluminum-foil pan (this pan goes to catch all the delicious meat juices so that you could make gravy). Place the pot at the grill, near the dome, and smoke within instant-study thermometer registers 130° to 135° F. Make positive to insert the controller away from the bone. Usually, this takes approximately 4 hours; however, begin to test after 2½ hours.

4. Transfer the roast to a slicing board, tent with foil, and permit relaxation for at least half-hour to let the juices settle. If you wish, make a small pan gravy (see left) out of the drippings. Carve the meat into thin slices and arrange on a warm platter. Serve immediately with horseradish sauce and the gravy.

GILROY SMOKED TRI-TIP

On a trip along California's Coast Highway, I stopped at a convenience store/farmers' market near Gilroy, south of San Francisco. The store had a small grill serving local favorites, and tri-tip sandwiches were on the menu. I had heard a lot about this style of barbecue, sometimes referred to as Santa Maria barbecue, and was eager to try it. After about two bites, I was back in the kitchen, talking the cookout of his recipe. I think you will enjoy this change of pace on smoked beef. Tri-tip sometimes needs to be special ordered, but I've found that most of the price clubs have it regularly.

Serves: 8 to 10
Ingredients:
1 tri-tip roast (3 to 4 pounds)
1 tablespoon chili powder
1 teaspoon garlic salt
Small amounts of freshly ground black pepper
Your favorite fresh salsa and pinto beans cooked with bacon for serving
Recommended wood: Hickory; I usually say soaking doesn't matter, however soaking the wooden in beer for an hour brings a pleasant taste to the tri-tip.

Directions:
1. At least 1 hour earlier than cooking, get rid of the roast from the refrigerator. Season all aspects with the chili powder, garlic salt, and lots and masses of black pepper.
2. Light on a hearth inside the kamado grill by using your favorite method. After about 10 minutes, close the dome and open the top and decrease dampers all the way. When the temperature reaches 300° F, place the wood chunks around the hearth and upload any add-ons essential for smoking on your unique grill, alongside the grill rack. Close the dome, allow the temperature to build lower back to among 200° and 250° F, and watch for a bit
3. Place the roast on the grill and smoke until an instant-study thermometer registers among 130° and 140° F, approximately 2 hours. Transfer the roast to a slicing board, tent with aluminum foil, and let relaxation for 15 minutes. Slice very thinly against the grain. Arrange on a platter and pour any gathered juice over the top. Serve with salsa and pinto beans.

HUGH LYNN'S TEXAS BRISKET WITH AN ONION TWIST

Sugarland, Texas, is a hot spot of Texas-style beef brisket perfection, and fortunately for me, my friend Hugh Lynn is a native of the region. Hugh has somehow managed to have all his work assignments in cities with excellent barbecue culture: Austin, Kansas City, Raleigh, and now Memphis. Hugh and his wife, Jean, taught me how good a beef brisket could be—quite a feat considering I'm a pork shoulder-loving North Carolinian. Hugh believes you should be gentle with your seasoning and keep the fire low. With a kamado, draft control is so precise you should never, ever end up with a tough, dried- out the brisket. One of the secrets to Hugh's brisket success is that he adds onion quarters to the fire. Not only will it drive you insane with the delicious smell, but it also imparts another layer of flavor to the finished brisket.

Even with the kamado, smoking brisket is a real commitment of time, so I always cook two at a time and throw one in the freezer.

Serves: 12, twice
Ingredients:
2 (5- to 6-pound) beef briskets
12 cloves garlic, thinly sliced
2 tablespoons Texas Brisket Rub
4 large onions, quartered
Recommended wood: Mesquite

Directions:
1. Using a knife, cut small slits into both briskets and slide a slice of garlic into every slit. Sprinkle every brisket with one tablespoon of the brisket rub and paintings it into the meat. Let sit at room temperature till you're ready to cook.
2. Light a fire in the kamado grill the usage of your preferred method. After approximately 10 minutes, near the dome and open the higher and decrease dampers, all of the manners. When the temperature reaches 300° F, place the timber chunks and the onions around the fire and add any accessories vital for smoking on your

precise grill, along with the grill rack. Close the dome, let the temperature come lower back to among 200° and 250° F, and watch for a touch smoke to accumulate. Adjust the dampers to keep the heat on this range.
3. Place the briskets on a rack in a drip pan, then place the container at the grill grate; the pot will trap the drippings that are top for making sauce or seasoning baked beans. Smoke the briskets for six to eight hours. After 6 hours, test the meat at its thickest factor with an instant-examine thermometer; 180° F is where you want to be.
4. Remove the briskets from the grill and wrap each in aluminum foil. Let one brisket cool completely, then wrap it once more in foil and freeze it; it will preserve up to a few months. (To reheat, let it thaw overnight in the refrigerator, then placed it in a preheated 350° F oven until warmed through, approximately half-hour.) Let the alternative brisket rest for 15 to 20 minutes, then slice thinly throughout the grain and serve. Pour any gathered juices over the beef. Serve the sauce on the aspect.

SWEET JEWISH-STYLE BRISKET

This recipe is based on my high school buddy Steve Grossman's mother's recipe. I always jumped at the chance to eat with the Grossmans; their food was so different from my mother's Southern fare. His mom would braise this dish, but I found a way to smoke it and still have a moist brisket and gravy.

Ingredients:

½ cup olive oil
½ cup cola
½ cup dry red wine
½ cup honey
5 tablespoons ketchup
2 cups finely chopped onions
½ teaspoon dry mustard, like Colman's
½ teaspoon smoked paprika
1 (5- to 7-pound) beef brisket
3 tablespoons unsalted butter or "pauvre" margarine
3 tablespoons gravy flour or all-purpose flour
Kosher salt and freshly ground black pepper
Recommended wood: Cherry or wine barrel chunks

Directions:

1. In a medium bowl, whisk the oil, cola, wine, honey, ketchup, onions, mustard, and paprika together.

2. Place the brisket in a 2½-gallon zip-pinnacle plastic bag or another container massive sufficient to hold it. Pour within the marinade and squish the whole thing around. Seal the bag or cowl the field and marinate overnight inside the refrigerator, turning the bag or brisket over occasionally. About an hour earlier than smoking, remove the brisket from the marinade; reserve the marinade.

3. Light on a fireplace inside the kamado grill through the usage of your favorite method. After about 10 minutes, near the dome and open the upper and decrease dampers all the way. When the temperature reaches 300° F, position the timber chunks around the hearth and upload any add-ons vital for smoking on your unique grill, along with the grill rack.

Close the dome, permit the temperature to build returned to among 200° and 250° F, and watch for a little smoke to accumulate.

4. Place the brisket on a rack in a drip pan, then location the container at the grill grate; the pot will capture the drippings, which might be top for making sauce or seasoning baked.

5. Close the dome and smoke for 5 to 6 hours, till an instant-study thermometer inserted at its thickest point reads 180° F. Remove the brisket from the grill and allow cooling. When cool, trim off the dense fats layer, if preferred. Wrap the brisket in aluminum foil and refrigerate overnight (believe me, you want to do this; the brisket flavor gets even better). Also, chill the brisket drippings and marinade.

6. Preheat the oven to 350° F., then reheat the brisket (still wrapped in foil) for about 20 minutes (until heated all of the manners through). While the brisket reheats, make the gravy if you like (and I extraordinarily recommend that you do). Melt the butter in a small saucepan over medium heat. Add the flour and whisk for 3 to 4 minutes. Very slowly and whisking constantly, upload the reserved marinade and drippings from the beef. Cook, stirring, until the gravy thickens for your liking, then taste and season with salt and pepper. Keep heat.

7. Slice the reheated brisket against the grain into thin slices and serve with the gravy poured over.

JAPANESE NEGIMAKI ROLL WITH LEMON DIPPING SAUCE

This is a reworking of the classic Japanese appetizer into a main course, and it is doggone good eating. Serve it over Japanese noodles or sushi rice, if you like, with some pickled ginger on the side. Ponzu is a citrus-flavored soy sauce; you can find it, and the other Japanese ingredients called for in the Asian sections of the largest supermarkets.

Serves: 6
Ingredients:
1 (3-pound) center-cut section beef tenderloin
2 tablespoons prepared wasabi paste
2 tablespoons good-quality mayonnaise 4 green onions, trimmed
4 pencil-thin asparagus spears, woody bottoms snapped off
½ cup shredded carrots Kitchen twine 1½ cup ponzu sauce
½ cup fresh lemon juice
½ cup tamari
½ cup of rice wine vinegar
½ cup mirin (sweet rice wine)
1 teaspoon toasted sesame oil
Shichimi (Japanese pepper blend), homemade or store-bought Teriyaki sauce as needed to glaze
Toasted sesame seeds (toast yourself in a dry skillet over medium heat, or you can buy already-toasted sesame seeds)

Directions:
1. Cut the tenderloin nearly in half lengthwise. On every side do another cut so that the piece of meat begins to put flat like a book.
2. In a small bowl, whisk the wasabi and mayonnaise collectively and unfold over the cut surfaces of the beef. Put the onions on the pinnacle of the meat so that the white and green alternate. Do the same with the asparagus then sprinkle the carrots over the top. Roll the beef up like a jellyroll and tie with kitchen cord at 1-inch intervals. Pour the ponzu into a 1-gallon zip-pinnacle plastic bag. Add the meat, seal, turn the bag over several times to coat the red meat with the ponzu, and refrigerate overnight.
3. Remove the meat from the marinade and pat dry at least 1 hour earlier than cooking. Make the dipping sauce through combining the lemon juice, tamari, vinegar, mirin, and sesame oil in a small bowl. Set aside at room temperature until geared up to serve.
4. Light on a hearth inside the kamado grill by the usage of your preferred method. After about 10 mins, vicinity the grill rack in position and near the dome, then open the upper and lower dampers all the way. When the temperature reaches 500° F, modify the dampers to keep the heat.
5. Five. Sprinkle the tenderloin generously with the Japanese pepper. Place the fillet on the grill, close the dome, and cook dinner for approximately five minutes per side to get an excellent sear. If necessary, regulate the dampers to drop the temperature right down to 425° F (it's likely already dropped

down significantly all through the searing) and preserve it there.

6. Insert the ceramic plate within the kamado and placed the tenderloin at the grill. Or positioned the tenderloin on a rack in a roasting pan and put on the grill. Close the dome and roast to your desired degree of doneness, 1 hour to one hour and 15 minutes for medium-rare (an inner temperature of 135° to 140° F).

7. Transfer the beef to a slicing board, brush generously with teriyaki sauce, and sprinkle with the sesame seeds. Let relaxation for 10 minutes. Remove the kitchen cord and reduce the roast into 1-inch-thick slices. Arrange on a platter and serve with the dipping sauce.

CHARRED WHOLE BEEF TENDERLOIN WITH ROMESCO SAUCE

Whole beef tenderloin is one of the simplest ways to feed a crowd. Spike it with slices of garlic that melt into the meat and use the kamado grill magic to keep the roast moist—there is no better way to prepare tenderloin. The tart Romesco sauce it's served with beats any steak sauce. And if there are any leftovers, you'll be able to enjoy the king of all roast beef sandwiches.

Serves 8 to 10
Ingredients:
1½ cup roasted red peppers
½ cup natural almonds
2 tablespoons red wine vinegar
1½ teaspoon red pepper flakes
2 cloves garlic, peeled
1 slice sourdough bread, crust removed
½ cup extra-virgin olive oil
1 whole beef tenderloin (about 6M pounds), silver skin removed
6 cloves garlic, thinly sliced
Kosher salt and freshly ground black pepper
12 green onions, trimmed
Directions:
1. Place the roasted peppers, almonds, vinegar, pink pepper flakes, whole garlic cloves, and bread in a blender and pulse to combine. With the gadget running, upload the oil slowly and process till you have a mild, thick sauce. The Romesco sauce may be prepared a day ahead and refrigerated in an airtight container. Bring to room temperature before the usage.

2. Using a boning knife, reduce small slits into the beef tenderloin and slide inside the slices of garlic. Liberally season with salt and pepper. Let relaxation at room temperature for as a minimum forty-five mins before cooking.

3. Light on fire in the kamado grill using your favored method. After approximately 10 mins, position the grill rack in position, close the dome, and open the upper and decrease dampers all the way. When the temperature reaches 500° F, adjust the dampers to preserve the heat.

4. Place the tenderloin at the grill, near the dome, and sear for five mins in line with side.

5. Insert the ceramic plate within the kamado and placed the tenderloin at the grill. Or placed the fillet on a rack in a roasting pan and put the container on the grill. Throw the green onions at the stand as well. Close the dome. The temperature may have dropped to around 425° to

450° F; modify the vents to hold that temperature and preserve to roast to your preferred diploma of doneness, 1 hour to 1 hour and 15 mins for medium-rare (an inner temperature of 135° to 140° F).

6. Transfer the tenderloin to a platter and allow relaxation for at least 15 mins. To serve, slice, set up the inexperienced onions with the red meat, and spoon the Romesco sauce over everything. This dish is tasty heat or at room temperature.

MR. PAYNE'S POT ROAST

The high school sweetheart's dad is the force behind this recipe. His classic was relatively straightforward and simple, and I've made only a few tweaks. I added the honey and chives, making an already-tasty result even more delicious. I've also changed up Mr. Payne's method. He would cook this roast over direct heat, and I remember him fighting and cussing at his fire as he tried not to char the outside of the roast. Considering how much sugar is in the French dressing, it was hard not to do. I've taken a different approach by charring the roast slightly (which is key to this roast's great flavor) over direct flame and then finishing it over indirect heat.

Serves 6
Ingredients:
1 (3-pound) boneless chuck roast
1 (16-ounce) bottle California French dressing
Kosher salt and freshly ground black pepper
1 tablespoon honey
1 tablespoon chopped fresh chives

Pumpernickel bread for serving (optional)
Directions:
1. Place the roast in a 1-gallon zip-top plastic bag. Pour off Y cup of the dressing and set it aside. Preserve the sauce produced in a bottle into the container. Seal the bag and squish the sauce across the roast to coat it thoroughly. Refrigerate for as much as 24 hours.

2. Remove the roast from the bag and discardrd the marinade. Season liberally with salt and pepper. Let stand at room temperature for 30 mins.

3. Light a fire inside the kamado grill the use of your favored method. After approximately 10 minutes, location the grill rack in position, near the dome, and open the upper and decrease dampers all the way. When the temperature reaches 500° F, regulate the dampers to hold the heat.

4. Place the roast at the grill, near the dome, and sear for five minutes in keeping with aspect. Remove the roast from the rack.

5. Insert the ceramic plate in the kamado and placed the roast on the grill. The alternative, put the roast on a rack in a roasting pan and positioned the container on the grill. Close the dome and adjust the dampers for a grill temperature of 375° to 400° F. Roast till the internal temperature at the thickest point is 175° F, approximately 1½ hours.

6. Transfer the roast to a reducing board. Drizzle with the honey and sprinkle with the chives. Let rest for 15 minutes, then slice thinly across the grain. Serve on a platter or make sandwiches with it using the pumpernickel bread.

STEAKHOUSE ROAST

I grew up in a home where we "enjoyed" a dry, overcooked eye of round roast every Sunday for lunch. This way is the antithesis of that roast. Garlicky and vibrant, with the unmatched flavor of a New York Strip steak, it's great for Sunday dinner or a party, and the leftovers make killer sandwiches, as well as being delicious served over a salad. This kind of roast is usually available at price clubs, but if not, ask your butcher to cut you one. Try it

Serves 6 to 8
Ingredients:
1 tablespoon Canadian-Style Steak Seasoning
1 tablespoon garlic paste (about 8 cloves garlic, smashed and worked into a dough, or prepared garlic paste in a tube, which can be found in the produce section)
1 tablespoon Worcestershire sauce
1 teaspoon Dijon mustard
1 (3- to 4-pound) New York strip loin roast Horseradish or steak sauce for serving.
Directions:
1. In a small bowl, combine the steak seasoning, garlic, Worcestershire, and mustard and rubdown the combination into the roast. Set the roast on a rack in a roasting pan and let stand at room temperature for an hour.
2. Light a hearth within the kamado grill the use of your favorite method. After approximately 10 mins, put the grill rack in the role, close the dome, and open the top and lower dampers all of the ways. When the temperature reaches 500° F, alter the

dampers to hold the temperatures.
3. Insert the ceramic plate in the kamado and placed the roast at the grill. Or positioned the roast on a rack in a roasting pan and put the container on the grill. Close the dome and alter the dampers for a grill temperature of 450° F. Roast to your preferred diploma of doneness, 1½ to two hours for medium-rare (an internal temperature of 135° to 140° F).
4. Transfer the roast to a cutting board and permit relaxation for 15 minutes. Slice as you prefer (I like ½-inch-thick slices), arrange on a platter and serve with the sauces if favored.

BEST KAMADO GRILL RECIPES

HOMEMADE GARLIC BURGERS

Ingredients:
3 1/2 pounds 80/20 ground beef
2 1/2 tablespoons garlic powder
1 teaspoon kosher salt
1 teaspoon ground black pepper
Directions:
1. Fire up your grill to 400°F.
2. In a large mixing bowl, integrate ground red meat, garlic powder, salt, and pepper.
3. Using a half-cup measuring cup, scoop out the ground red meat mixture and shape the meat into hamburger patties.
4. Grill over direct heat at 400°F for 7-10 mins for side, and pull when internal temperature reaches around 150°F or while

meat reaches your preferred temperature.

ARROWHEAD MOUNTAIN BURGERS

Ingredients:
3 ½ lbs. 80/20 ground beef
1 1/2 teaspoons sage
1 teaspoon garlic powder
1/2 teaspoon thyme
2 teaspoons salt
1 teaspoon pepper

Directions:
1. Combine spices in a small blending bowl and whisk collectively.
2. In a huge blending bowl, upload the ground red meat and about three-fourths of the spices. Mix to mix nicely.
3. Shape meat into hamburger patties and sprinkle each aspect of burger with a touch bit of the leftover spice mixture (makes about eight patties).
4. Grill those over direct warmness at 450 F for 7-10 mins according to the aspect, or until internal temperature reaches 160F.

MARINATED GRILLED STEAK FAJITAS WITH HOMEMADE CHIMICHURRI SAUCE

Ingredients:
2 lbs. cab top sirloin strip steak
1/3 cup olive oil
juice of 1 lime
2 teaspoons garlic powder
1 tablespoon onion powder
1/2 teaspoon ground nutmeg
1 teaspoon salt

Directions:

Directions:
1. Whisk collectively olive oil, lime juice, and spices.
2. Place meat in a shallow dish and pour marinade on top of it. Let steak marinate on this overnight in the refrigerator or at least an hour.
3. Preheat grill to 450-500F.
4. Grill steak approximately 5 minutes in line with the side (or till the inner temperature reaches 145F).
5. Remove from grill and let rest about ten minutes.
6. Serve with self-made chimichurri sauce.

CILANTRO-LIME STEAK FAJITAS

A spicy blend of flavors paired with refreshing lime and cilantro will make this fajita recipe your new favorite.

Ingredients:
1-pound beef steak strips
1/3 cup olive oil
1/2 cup freshly squeezed lime juice
1/2 cup fresh cilantro, chopped
2 cloves garlic, minced
1 teaspoon honey
1/2 teaspoon chili powder
1 teaspoon cayenne pepper
1 teaspoon red chili flakes
1 teaspoon salt
3 bell peppers, sliced
1 onion, sliced
8 flour tortillas
Extra cilantro leaves to garnis
Guacamole (optional) to serve

Directions:
1. Whisk collectively olive oil, lime juice, cilantro, garlic, honey, and spices.

Reserve approximately one-fourth of the marinade and refrigerate.

2. Place meat in a shallow dish and pour closing three-fourths of the marinade on the pinnacle of it. Let beef marinate in this overnight inside the refrigerator, or as a minimum an hour.

3. Preheat grill to 450°F-500°F.

4. Slice bell peppers and onion and put in a grilling basket or tin foil packet with a bit olive oil and garlic salt.

5. Grill steak approximately five minutes per facet (or until internal temperature reaches 145°F). Brush reserved marinade on after flipping. Once finished, do away with from grill, cover with foil, and let rest.

6. Then, prepare the peppers and onion and grill at 450°F-500°F, for about 10 mins.

7. Finally, prepare the fajitas, warming tortilla 10 seconds, and assembling with your garnishing and seasoning with greater cilantro, guacamole, and your favorite hot sauce.

HAMBURGER PATTIE RECIPE

Take your burgers to the next level with this homemade hamburger patties recipe.

Ingredients:
3 teaspoons paprika
2 1/2 pounds ground beef
3 teaspoons ground black pepper
2 teaspoons fine sea salt
1 teaspoon dark brown sugar
1 teaspoon garlic powder
1 teaspoon onion powder
Directions:

Directions:
1. Combine all of the spices in a small blending bowl and whisk collectively.

2. In a big mixing bowl, add the ground pork and about three-fourths of the spices. Mix to combine correctly.

3. Shape meat into hamburger patties and sprinkle both aspects of burger with a little bit of leftover spice aggregate (makes approximately eight patties).

4. Grill those over direct warmness at 450°F for 7-10 minutes in keeping with side, relying on how nicely cooked you want them.

BBQ HOT SAUCE BLUE CHEESE BURGERS

Ingredients:
2 pounds ground beef
1/2 cup BBQ sauce
1 tablespoon hot pepper sauce
2/3 cup blue cheese crumbles, plus more for garnish
1 bunch scallions, chopped
1 teaspoon garlic powder
1 teaspoon kosher salt
Directions:
1. Whisk together BBQ sauce and hot pepper suce and set aside.

2. In a medium mixing bowl, integrate ground red meat, 2 tablespoons of BBQ hot pepper sauce aggregate, blue cheese crumbles, scallions, garlic powder, and salt.

3. Using a 1/3 measuring cup as a guide, shape pork into eight-10 patties. Brush tops of burgers with BBQ sauce mixture.

4. Preheat grill to 400F. Place burgers on grill over direct warmth, sauce side

down, and brush tops of burgers with last sauce. Grill, turning once, until cooked through, approximately 10 minutes, or till the inner temperature reads 160F.

LIME-CILANTRO VINAIGRETTE

This lime-cilantro vinaigrette is light and refreshing. Drizzle it on vegetables, salads, or use it as a marinade.

Ingredients:
1/4 cup lime juice (about 2 limes)
1/4 cup white wine vinegar
4 cloves garlic, minced
2 teaspoons sugar
1/2 teaspoon salt
1 cup of vegetable oil
1/2 cup fresh cilantro, chopped

Directions:
1. Pulse lime juice, vinegar, garlic, sugar, and salt in a food processor several times.
2. With the meals processor nevertheless running, upload the oil in a constant stream. Add cilantro and pulse some times.
3. Transfer to a mason jar and refrigerate.
4. Serve on vegetables, salads, or use as a marinade.

RACHEL'S BBQ RUB

This dish is the perfect combination of sweet and spicy.

Ingredients:
1/2 cup brown sugar
1 tablespoon garlic powder
1 tablespoon paprika
2 teaspoons dry mustard
1 teaspoon chili powder

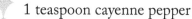

1 teaspoon cayenne pepper
1 teaspoon onion powder
1 teaspoon kosher salt
1 teaspoon black pepper

Directions:
1. Measure out spices in a medium mixing bowl and whisk collectively.
2. Rub on red meat.

EASY GRILLED RIBS

Ingredients:
2 racks pork loin ribs
BBQ Sauce
4 tablespoons unsalted butter, sliced
aluminum foil
BBQ RUB
1/2 cup brown sugar
1 tablespoon garlic powder
1 tablespoon paprika
2 teaspoons dry mustard
1 teaspoon chili powder
1 teaspoon cayenne pepper
1 teaspoon onion powder
1 teaspoon black pepper

Directions:
1. Remove membranes from beef backs and trim extra fat.
2. In a medium blending bowl, whisk BBQ rub collectively. Rub it all over beef backs.
3. Preheat grill to 350°-400°F and set warmth deflector in the area.
4. Place ribs on grates and grill on oblique warmth for 45 mins.
5. Wrap ribs in foil and area butter slices on the pinnacle. Grill for any other 30 mins.
6. Remove the foil and coat ribs with BBQ sauce. Put meat on the grill, close both grill vents, and permit the beef to rest and

BBQ sauce to get satisfactory and tacky for 20-30 minutes.

COUNTRY DIJON-BALSAMIC GRILLED PORK TENDERLOIN

Ingredients:
2 1/2 pounds' pork tenderloin
1/4 cup country Dijon mustard
3 tablespoons balsamic vinegar
2 tablespoons olive oil
1/4 cup brown sugar
2 cloves garlic, minced
1 teaspoon salt
1/2 teaspoon ground black pepper

Directions:
1. Whisk marinade ingredients together.
2. Transfer to a zip lock bag with red meat tenderloin. Shake bag to marinate the meat and refrigerate as a minimum of two hours or as much as 24 hours.
3. Preheat grill to 250 ranges Fahrenheit.
4. Grill beef tenderloin over oblique heat till the internal temperature reaches 145F (about 45 mins).
5. Remove and permit rest for 10 minutes earlier than reducing and serving. Enjoy!

HONEY-APPLE BBQ GLAZED RIBS

Ingredients:
2 racks pork loin backs
Rachel's BBQ Rub
1 batch Honey-Apple BBQ Sauce

Directions:
1. Remove membranes from pork backs and trim excess fat.
2. In a medium blending bowl, whisk

Rachel's BBQ Rub collectively. Rub it throughout pork backs.
3. Preheat grill to 350°-400°F and set warmness deflector in place.
4. Place ribs on grates and grill on indirect warmth for 1 hour 45 mins.
5. While ribs are grilling, make a batch of Honey-Apple BBQ Sauce and set aside to use as basting.
6. Baste ribs with Honey-Apple BBQ Sauce and grill for every other 20 mins.
7. Baste ribs again, and grill for another 10 mins, or till the internal temperature reaches 190-195°F.
8. Remove ribs from grill and let relaxation 15 minutes earlier than serving.

HONEY-GARLIC ORANGE GRILLED CHICKEN THIGHS

Ingredients:
4 1/2 pounds boneless, skinless chicken thighs
1 tablespoon salt
2 tablespoons garlic powder The Glaze
1 cup bone broth (chicken broth or water work too)
1 cup honey
juice and zest of 1 orange
6 garlic cloves, pressed
1 tablespoon coconut amino

Directions:
1. Mix garlic powder and salt in blending bowl. Coat chicken thighs in combination, area in a zip lock bag, and refrigerate.
2. Preheat grill to 450°F.
3. Meanwhile, make the glaze by whisking components collectively in a

medium saucepan over medium-high heat till boiling. Let simmer 10 minutes and dispose of from warmness and allow thickening.

4. Reserve a portion of glaze to apply later in the stir fry.

5. Grill hen thighs over indirect heat at 450° F for 30 minutes, glaze and flip, and grill for about some other 15 minutes, or till the inner temperature of the chook reaches 180°F.

6. Let bird relaxation 10-15 mins.

Notes

1. The Glaze is not the thickest; however, it ought to thicken up a little bit as soon as cooled. Sometimes I like to make the glaze in advance of time and refrigerate it to assist it in thickening.

COCONUT AMINOS

You can replace soy sauce for the coconut amino if you aren't following the autoimmune protocol.

Ingredients:

3 1/2 pounds' chicken drumsticks or wings
2 1/2 tablespoons arrowroot powder
1 tablespoon cream of tartar
1/2 teaspoon baking soda
1 teaspoon garlic powder
1 teaspoon onion powder
1 teaspoon salt

The Glaze

1/2 cup honey
3 tablespoons coconut amino
4 garlic cloves, minced
1/4 cup water

Directions:

1. Whisk spices, baking soda, cream of tartar, and arrowroot powder collectively.

2. Toss bird into the coat and switch to a zip-lock plastic bag. Refrigerate for at the least hours or as much as 24 hours.

3. Preheat grill to 450°F. Grill bird wings on indirect warmness for 30 minutes.

4. Meanwhile, warm the honey with water, coconut amino, garlic, and a pinch of salt in a small saucepan over medium-excessive warmness. Turn heat down to low as soon as it starts evolved to simmer and let simmer for 5 minutes. Remove from warmness and let cool.

5. Flip fowl wings and glazed with sauce. Grill for any other 15 minutes at 450°F and get rid of once the inner temperature reaches around 170-180°F or at least 165°F.

Notes

This recipe makes use of wholesome substitutes to be compliant with the autoimmune protocol, however, may be made using traditional ingredients as well. Feel free to apply a half cup of flour in the area of the arrowroot powder, one teaspoon baking powder in the vicinity of the baking soda and cream of tartar, and soy sauce in the region of the coconut amino.

HERBED OLIVE OIL GRILLED THANKSGIVING TURKEY

Ingredients:

15 pounds' fresh turkey
2 tablespoons dry parsley
2 tablespoons crushed thyme
1 teaspoon paprika
1 teaspoon ground black pepper
2 teaspoons kosher salt
1 V cups extra virgin olive oil

Directions:

1. Rinse the turkey under bloodless water

and pat dry.

2. Mix the parsley, thyme, paprika, salt, and pepper. Stir in olive oil till combined.

3. Brush herbed olive oil all over turkey.

4. Preheat grill to 350 degrees F.

5. Put the turkey on a rack in a grill. Roast on indirect warmth until the skin is golden brown and inner temperature registers 165 degrees F, approximately 15 mins in keeping with the pound. Transfer to a reducing board and permit the rest 30 minutes earlier than carving.

TURKEY APPLE BURGERS

Ingredients:

3 1/2 pounds ground turkey

1 apple, finely minced

1 teaspoon garlic powder

1 1/2 teaspoons onion powder

1 teaspoon oregano

1 teaspoon salt

1 teaspoon pepper

Directions:

1. Preheat grill to 450 F.

2. Meanwhile, make patties by using combining turkey, apple, and spices in a mixing bowl. Mix very well together with your hands. Use a one-1/2 cup as your guide and shape meat patties.

3. Grill on direct warmness at 450F for around 30 minutes, flipping 1/2 way through. Grill till internal meat temperature reaches 165F.

4. Remove patties and permit relaxation five mins earlier than serving.

PARSLEY-THYME GRILLED TURKEY BURGERS

Ingredients:

1-pound ground turkey

1 teaspoon dry parsley

1/2 teaspoon crushed thyme

1/2 teaspoon garlic powder

1/2 teaspoon kosher salt

1/2 teaspoon ground black pepper

Directions:

1. Preheat grill to 450° F.

2. Meanwhile, make patties utilizing combining turkey and spices in the blending bowl. Mix thorough together with your hands. Form about four meat patties and press flat, patties will reduce and flatten up a piece on the grill.

3. Grill on direct warmth at 450° F for round 30 minutes, flipping half manner through. Check internal meat temperature before disposing of from the rack, and it ought to be 165° F.

4. Remove patties and let relaxation 5 minutes before serving.

THANKSGIVING STUFFING WITH PARSLEY-THYME GRILLED TURKEY BURGER

Ingredients:

1 French loaf bread, cubed

12 tablespoons butter (1.5 sticks)

1 onion, diced

1 1/2 cups chopped celery (about 3 stalks)

2 large carrots, peeled and chopped

6 ounces' baby Bella mushrooms, chopped

1 clove garlic, minced

1 -1.5 cups chicken broth
1/2 teaspoon thyme
1/2 teaspoon parsley
Salt and pepper
1 pound grilled parsley-thyme burgers, cubed

Directions:

1. Preheat oven to 350° F. Place cubed French bread onto a large jelly roll baking sheet. Bake for 20 minutes.

2. Melt butter in a large saucepan over medium excessive heat. Sauté onions, celery, carrots and mushrooms for 10-15 mins, or till vegetables are tender. Add salt and pepper. Stir in garlic and cook for some other minute, then pour in chook broth, parsley, and thyme. Stir and simmer.

3. Add grilled parsley-thyme burgers to the vegetable combination. Place bread cubes in a huge blending bowl and pour mix over cubes lightly stirring, season to taste, and pour the mixture in greased 9x13 baking dish. Bake at 350°F for 25-30 minutes until golden brown. Remove from the oven.

DELICIOUS GRILLED VEGETABLES

Grilled Vegetables Delicious grilled vegetables are easy to make and packed with nutrients. Enjoy them directly off the grill or drizzle with lime-cilantro vinaigrette for added flavor.

Ingredients:

1/2 head red cabbage, sliced
1 sweet potato, peeled and sliced
1/2 red onion, chopped
1 red bell pepper, sliced

1/2 pound Brussel sprouts, trimmed and halved
1 tablespoon extra-virgin olive oil
salt
pepper

Directions:

1. Rinse veggies below cold, running water. Prepare greens and arrange them in foil pan.

2. Preheat grill to 450F and place heat deflector in a kamado. Grill on oblique warmth for 30 minutes, or until roasted for your liking.

3. Serve at once or drizzle with lime-cilantro vinaigrette.

MAPLE GLAZED CARROTS

Ingredients:

1 pound carrots, peeled and chopped
2 teaspoons extra virgin olive oil
3 tablespoons pure maple syrup
2 tablespoons white wine vinegar
1/2 teaspoon freshly ground black pepper
1/4 teaspoon ground cinnamon

Directions:

1. Preheat grill to 450° F.

2. Wash, peel, and chop carrots.

3. In a bowl, combine olive oil, maple syrup, white wine vinegar, pepper, and cinnamon. Stir in carrots until well coated.

4. Set forged iron pan in kamado and permit to preheat.

5. Transfer carrots to preheated forged iron pan.

6. Grill at 450° F over oblique heat for about 45 minutes to an hour, or until the carrots become smooth.

BACON-WRAPPED ASPARAGUS

The Asparagus is wrapped with a slice of thick-cut bacon straight off the grill.

Ingredients:

1-pound thick bacon
1 bundle fresh asparagus stalks
2 tablespoons extra virgin olive oil
1 teaspoon ground black pepper

Directions:

1. Preheat grill to 400F.
2. Rinse asparagus and trim ends of stalks.
3. Group asparagus in bundles of three-five spears.
4. Place bacon-wrapped asparagus bundles in foil pan. Drizzle with olive oil and sprinkle with pepper.
5. Grill on direct warmness approximately 10 mins consistent with side, or until desired crispiness.

THE BEST PULLED PORK

Juicy sweet and spicy rubbed meat with flavorful, crispy bark makes this smoked pulled pork recipe phenomenal.

Ingredients:

8 pounds' pork shoulder
buns
BBQ sauce
wood chips, if desired BBQ Rub
1/2 cup brown sugar
1 tablespoon garlic powder
1 tablespoon paprika
2 teaspoons dry mustard
1 teaspoon chili powder
1 teaspoon cayenne pepper
1 teaspoon onion powder
1 teaspoon black pepper

Directions:

1. In a medium blending bowl, whisk BBQ rub collectively. Rub all of it over pork shoulder.
2. Preheat grill to 250°F and load with masses of clean charcoal.
3. Place pork shoulder on a roasting rack and place it on the grill. Add wooden chips if the usage of them (keep to add every hour if you want a strong flavor.)
4. Grill on indirect warmth for 16 hours or until the inner temperature of the meat reaches 190-195° F.
5. Remove from grill, wrap in butcher paper or foil, and let rest for an excellent half-hour.
6. Shred and experience on buns with your favored BBQ sauce.

Notes

For the first-rate flavor, rub your beef shoulder 24 hours earlier than smoking it. Grill for around 1.5-2 hours consistent with a pound of meat, adding a 1-hour time cushion. Be kind to the time if you are unsure.

Typically, there is a "stall zone" around 165°F to 180°F.

If you end early, wrap your meat in butcher paper or foil, then cover that during a towel, and place inside a cooler. Meat should stay heat for hours.

HONEY BBQ GRILLED CHICKEN

Ingredients:

3 1/2 pounds boneless, skinless chicken breasts
1 cup BBQ sauce

2/3 cup honey
1 tablespoon white wine vinegar
1 teaspoon garlic powder
1/2 teaspoon cayenne pepper
1 teaspoon salt
1 teaspoon pepper

Directions:
1. Whisk collectively and marinade the ingredients.
2. Place bird in zip lock bag, pour in marinade, reserving a few for basting. Let marinate in the refrigerator for up to two hours.
3. While chook is marinating, preheat grill.
4. Grill on oblique warmness around 400-450° F for about 40 mins, flip and baste half of way through. Grill until inner temperature reaches 165-175° F. Remove the hen from grill and brush with any closing marinade. Let rest 10 minutes.

SPICY MARINATED CHICKEN THIGHS

Ingredients:
2 1/2 pounds' chicken thighs
4 garlic cloves, minced
1/2 cup soy sauce
1/3 cup apple cider vinegar
1/3 cup lime juice (about 2 limes)
1/4 cup sriracha chili sauce
1 tablespoon honey
1 teaspoon ground black pepper
1/2 teaspoon salt

Directions:
1. Whisk marinade ingredients collectively. Transfer it to a marinade in a plastic zip-lock bag.
2. Add bird thighs to bag. Toss to coat. Refrigerate as a minimum of 2 hours (or

up to three hours).
3. Preheat grill to 450F. Grill on indirect warmth for 35-40 mins, or till internal temperature hits 165F.
NOTES
This recipe is mildly spicy. For introduced warmness, increase the quantity of sriracha chili sauce to 1/three cup and add one teaspoon pink pepper flakes.

SOUTHERN STYLE MEATLOAF

Ingredients:
2 lbs. Ground Beef
1 Onion, minced
1 Green Pepper, minced
1 Egg
2/3 cup Vision Grills BBQ Sauce (Kansas City Style Recommended)
3 tbsp. Vision Grills BBQ Rub (Kansas City Style Recommended)
1/2 cup Italian Bread Crumbs
1 tsp Salt
1/2 tsp Black Pepper
1/2 tsp Garlic Salt
1/4 tsp Cayenne Pepper
1 tbsp. Worcestershire Sauce
1 tbsp. Hot Sauce
1/4 tsp Oregano
1/4 tsp Basil
1/3 cup 2% Milk
Meatloaf Done
Directions:
1. In a massive bowl, upload the Ground Beef, Onion, Pepper, Garlic, Egg, 1/three cup BBQ Sauce, Italian Bread Crumbs, Salt, Pepper, Cayenne, Basil, Oregano, and Milk
2. Using your hands, knead the beef

mixture until the whole lot is nicely combined

3. Mold the beef right into a loaf shape and sprinkle the pinnacle with BBQ Rub
4. Startup your Vision Kamado and get it to 350°F.
5. Place meatloaf in Vision Kamado once it reaches 350°F
6. Brush with 1/three cup of BBQ Sauce after the meatloaf reaches 140°F (about an hour and a 1/2 in)
7. Remove while the internal temperature is at 160°F (approximately two hours).

CAROLINA STYLE SHRIMP

Ingredients:
2 half-size disposable aluminum pans
Vision Grills Carolina Style Dry Rub
Vision Grills Carolina Style BBQ Sauce
2 lbs. of thawed and deveined shrimp
1/2 lemon
2 sticks salted butter

Directions:
1. Heat your Vision Grill as much as 250°F
2. Pour 2 lbs. Of shrimp into one pan
3. Pour sufficient Vision Grills Carolina BBQ Sauce to coat the bottom of the second one pan
4. Pour a generous coating of Vision Grills Carolina Style Dry Rub onto the shrimp
5. Hand toss the shrimp to calmly coat in the rub, upload more seasoning if needed
6. Move over the shrimp into the BBQ lined pan
7. Squeeze a 1/2 of a lemon onto the shrimp
8. Place sticks of unsalted butter on top of the shrimp

9. Place the container of shrimp without delay onto your grill rack
10. Close your grill and cook the shrimp for approximately 35 mins or till cooked to at least 120°F
11. Remove the pan from the shelf with a warning and enjoy it!

GRILLED CHICKEN QUESADILLA SANDWICH

Ingredients:
4 Chicken Breasts
1 package Taco Seasoning
1 Green Bell Pepper
1 Red Bell Pepper
1 Red Onion
2 cups Monterey Jack Cheese
4 Ciabatta Buns (sliced in half)
½ cup Margarine
1 Tbsp. Croix Valley Garlic Barbecue Booster
1 cup Sour Cream
2 Tbsp. Chipotle in Adobo Sauce
1 cup Ajvar Relish (Eastern European relish of garlic, peppers, and eggplant)
1 Tbsp. Olive Oil
1 head Iceberg Lettuce, shredded
1 medium Tomato, diced.

Directions:
1. Lightly oil hen breasts and coast generously with Taco Seasoning.
2. Grill cook over the medium grill (about 3500F) until internal temperature reaches 1650F. Let relaxation 5 minutes then slice into strips.
3. Julienne peppers and onion. Fry in oil until greens begin to brown. Cover and set aside.

4. Make four piles of chook (as flat as possible) on the baking sheet. Then, put in the top the fried vegetables, ½ cup of cheese, a sprint of taco seasoning. Transfer to blanketed grill and cook till cheese begins to brown.

5. Combine margarine and garlic seasoning. Blend properly.

6. Spread margarine garlic mixture on internal of ciabatta buns. Grill till they begin to brown.

7. Combine buttercream and chipotle in adobo sauce. Blend well.

8. Spread Ajvar savor on inner of backside bun.

9. Place chicken/vegetable/cheese stacks on top of Ajvar delight.

10. Top with shredded lettuce and diced tomato.

11. Spread the chipotle mixture on internal of pinnacle bun and pinnacle off the sandwich.

12. Serve and enjoy!

SMOKED GEORGIA PEACH CHICKEN WINGS

Ingredients:
About 4-5 lbs. of Chicken Wings (separated into drums and flats)
4 Teaspoons of Kosher Salt
2 Teaspoons of Cracked Pepper
2 Teaspoons of Season Salt
3 Tablespoons of Smoked Paprika
1 Tablespoon of Chili Powder
1 Tablespoon of Garlic Powder
1 Teaspoon of Chipotle Chili Powder
1 Teaspoon of Mustard Powder
2 Tablespoons of Unsalted Butter
1/2-3/4 Cup of Peach Chutney (typically in a jelly aisle at store)
1 Tablespoon of Mild Flavored Molasses
1/2 Cup of BBQ Sauce - (Something not too sweet)
1/2 Buffalo Wing Sauce - (Whatever your favorite is)
1/2 Cup of Hot Sauce - (Again, your brand of choice)

Directions:
1. To make the rub, integrate the kosher salt, cracked pepper, season salt, smoked paprika, chili powder, garlic powder, chipotle chili powder, and mustard powder right into a bowl. The quantity of rub you need relies on what number of hen wings you're making. You want sufficient rub to coat both facets of each chicken wing calmly. The right place to begin is with about a teaspoon of each.

2. Cover the bird wings inside the rub and set aside.

3. Set the smoker to smoke with indirect heat and set the temperature to 225 ranges F. I commonly smoke mine over hickory wood. Once the smoker is in warmth, place the wings on and let it burn for one hour and thirty minutes.

4. To make the wing sauce, soften the butter in a medium-sized saucepan over medium heat. Once the butter has melted, upload the BBQ Sauce, hot sauce, buffalo sauce, and peach chutney (peach preserves). Cook until heated via and season with kosher salt.

5. Once the sauce is complete, and the wings are done, toss the sides in the sauce and enjoy.

in a jelly aisle at store)
1 Tablespoon of Mild Flavored Molasses
1/2 Cup of BBQ Sauce - (Something not too sweet)
1/2 Buffalo Wing Sauce - (Whatever your favorite is)
1/2 Cup of Hot Sauce - (Again, your brand of choice)

Directions:

1. To make the rub, integrate the kosher salt, cracked pepper, season salt, smoked paprika, chili powder, garlic powder, chipotle chili powder, and mustard powder right into a bowl. The quantity of rub you need relies on what number of hen wings you're making. You want sufficient rub to coat both facets of each chicken wing calmly. The right place to begin is with about a teaspoon of each.

2. Cover the bird wings inside the rub and set aside.

3. Set the smoker to smoke with indirect heat and set the temperature to 225 ranges F. I commonly smoke mine over hickory wood. Once the smoker is in warmth, place the wings on and let it burn for one hour and thirty minutes.

4. To make the wing sauce, soften the butter in a medium-sized saucepan over medium heat. Once the butter has melted, upload the BBQ Sauce, hot sauce, buffalo sauce, and peach chutney (peach preserves). Cook until heated via and season with kosher salt.

5. Once the sauce is complete, and the wings are done, toss the sides in the sauce and enjoy.

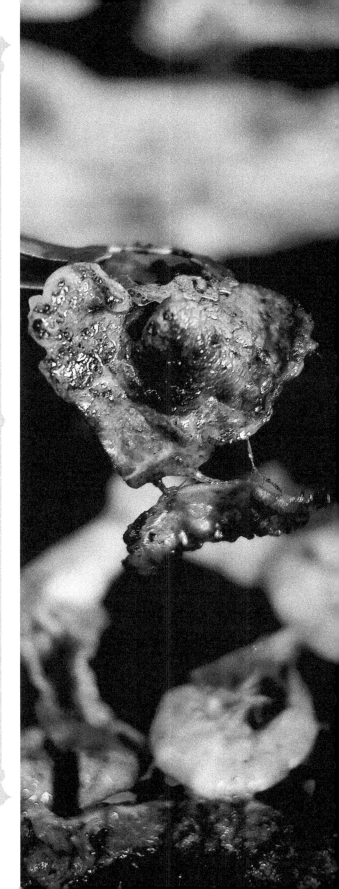

AFTERWORD

Conclusion First of all, I want to thank you for buying our book, which was the result of a long period of work for us.

We always try to give my best in our books to offer the reader the highest possible experience. All contents are enriched and analyzed in detail so that you can find the solutions you were looking for in our manuscripts.

We hope we have responded, even if in part, to your expectations.

We will be grateful if you could leave your own review at:
vancouverpress2020@gmail.com

This would be really important to us and our work. We promise that we will read your opinion with interest.

Here's your gift: https://bit.ly/VANCOUVERBBQ

A warm greeting, dear reader friend.

CPSIA information can be obtained
at www.ICGtesting.com
Printed in the USA
BVHW011736080221
599639BV00014B/1177